GW00645182

LIVERPOOL STREET TO CHINGFORD

J.E.Connor
Series editor Vic Mitchell

MP Middleton Press

Cover Photograph : Class N7 0-6-2T No 69602 is seen at Bethnal Green with a Liverpool Street - Chingford train in the 1950s. The nice wooden running-in board seen on the right is believed to have been removed soon after, when the station was provided with new British Railways-type signs. (A. Ingram Collection)

First published January 2003

ISBN 1 904474 01 2

© *Middleton Press*

Cover design Deborah Esher

Published by
Middleton Press
Easebourne Lane
Midhurst, West Sussex
GU29 9AZ
Tel: 01730 813169
Fax: 01730 812601

Layout and typesetting London Railway Record

Printed & bound by Biddles Ltd.
Guildford and King's Lynn

CONTENTS

ACKNOWLEDGEMENTS

Thanks as always to the usual London Railway Record team for their help in the preparation of this book, particularly John Crook, whose meticulous checking of historical facts has proved invaluable. I should also like to thank Ian Strugnell who has provided me with much useful information on signal boxes, gleaned by himself and a group of colleagues, from original sources. The map displayed overleaf was produced by Charlie Connor of Street Level Models.

GEOGRAPHICAL SETTING

The 10-mile long route is on the north flank of the Thames Valley and traverses mainly London Clay. It was initially largely rural, passing through small holdings and farmland. However, it was the cause of its own environmental transition to urban surroundings. It climbs from about 50ft above sea level to 180, the terminus being near the edge of Epping Forest.

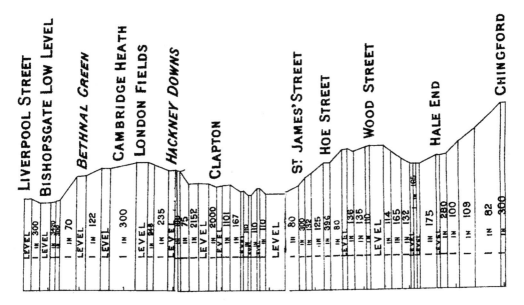

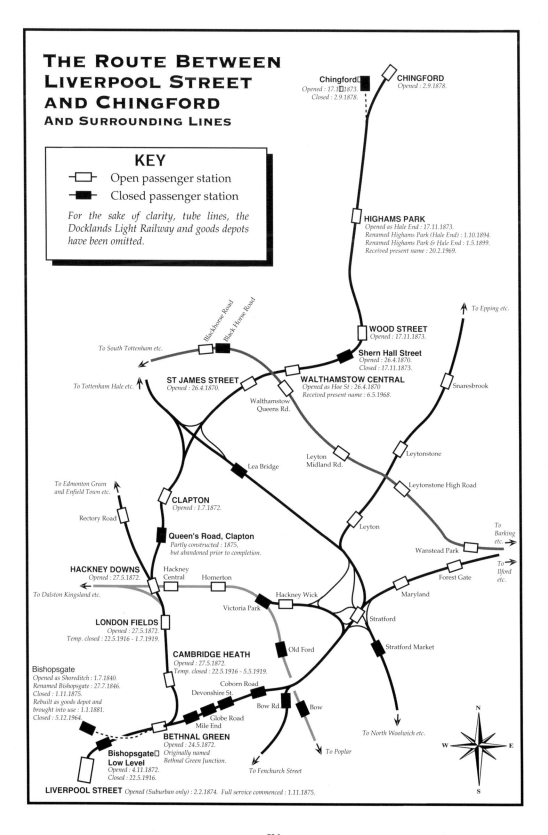

THE ROUTE BETWEEN LIVERPOOL STREET AND CHINGFORD
AND SURROUNDING LINES

KEY

▭ Open passenger station

■ Closed passenger station

For the sake of clarity, tube lines, the Docklands Light Railway and goods depots have been omitted.

Chingford
Opened : 17.11.1873.
Closed : 2.9.1878.

CHINGFORD
Opened : 2.9.1878.

HIGHAMS PARK
Opened as Hale End : 17.11.1873.
Renamed Highams Park (Hale End) : 1.10.1894.
Renamed Highams Park & Hale End : 1.5.1899.
Received present name : 20.2.1969.

To Epping etc.

Blackhorse Road

Black Horse Road

To South Tottenham etc.

To Tottenham Hale etc.

WOOD STREET
Opened : 17.11.1873.

Shern Hall Street
Opened : 26.4.1870.
Closed : 17.11.1873.

ST JAMES STREET
Opened : 26.4.1870.

WALTHAMSTOW CENTRAL
Opened as Hoe St : 26.4.1870.
Received present name : 6.5.1968.

Snaresbrook

Walthamstow
Queens Rd.

Leyton
Midland Rd.

Leytonstone

Lea Bridge

Leytonstone High Road

To Edmonton Green
and Enfield Town etc.

CLAPTON
Opened : 1.7.1872.

Leyton

Rectory Road

Queen's Road, Clapton
Partly constructed : 1875,
but abandoned prior to completion.

To
Barking
etc.

Wanstead Park

HACKNEY DOWNS
Opened : 27.5.1872.

Hackney
Central

Homerton

To
Ilford
etc.

Forest Gate

To Dalston Kingsland etc.

Hackney Wick

Maryland

Victoria Park

Stratford

LONDON FIELDS
Opened : 27.5.1872.
Temp. closed : 22.5.1916 - 1.7.1919.

Stratford Market

CAMBRIDGE HEATH
Opened : 27.5.1872.
Temp. closed : 22.5.1916 - 5.5.1919.

Old Ford

Bishopsgate
Opened as Shoreditch : 1.7.1840.
Renamed Bishopsgate : 27.7.1846.
Closed : 1.11.1875.
Rebuilt as goods depot and
brought into use : 1.1.1881.
Closed : 5.12.1964.

Coborn Road

Devonshire St.

Bow Rd.

Bow

Globe Road
Mile End

To North Woolwich etc.

BETHNAL GREEN
Opened : 24.5.1872.
Originally named
Bethnal Green Junction.

To Poplar

Bishopsgate
Low Level
Opened : 4.11.1872.
Closed : 22.5.1916.

To Fenchurch Street

LIVERPOOL STREET Opened (Suburban only) : 2.2.1874. Full service commenced : 1.11.1875.

N
W   E
S

HISTORICAL BACKGROUND

On 23rd June 1864, the Great Eastern Railway received Parliamentary Authority to construct a branch to High Beech in Epping Forest. This was to leave the existing Loughton line near Stratford and head northwards through Walthamstow. A month later, on 29th July, approval was given to construct an additional route to Walthamstow, which would branch off at Bethnal Green then continue by way of Hackney Downs and Clapton.

Financial constraints resulted in delays however and it seems that very little of the necessary work was carried out. The situation was so bad that a receiver was appointed during 1867, then two years later, in the summer of 1869, the GER decided to abandon the entire route from Stratford to High Beech. The Hackney Downs scheme remained alive however and the company duly sought powers to extend the route beyond Walthamstow to Chingford.

Work on this line had also virtually ground to a halt and for some time, the unfinished embankment ended abruptly on the west side of St. James Street. Progress was undeniably slow, but by opening a spur from Lea Bridge on the Cambridge line to Hall Farm Junction, it proved possible to introduce a service to and from Shern Hall Street, Walthamstow on 26th April 1870.

Around this time, the Great Eastern Railway was extremely busy in the London area, particularly at the City end where a new terminus was under construction.

The GER had been formed in 1862 by the amalgamation of the Eastern Counties Railway and various smaller companies. From the ECR it had inherited a terminus, originally called Shoreditch, but by then named Bishopsgate. This faced onto Shoreditch High Street and although rebuilt with an attractive Italianate frontage by the architect Sancton Wood in 1848-9, was still too small to deal with its burgeoning traffic. Added to this, it bordered on an area frequented by criminals and it seems that some passengers felt unsafe using it. Be this as it may, it was also some distance from the City business district, so this, together with its small capacity were the chief reasons for its demise.

The new terminus was constructed at Liverpool Street, but to reach this, the tracks had to descend a 1 in 70 incline from viaduct level near Bethnal Green, then pass beneath the original formation in deep brick-lined cutting. Before the line could be opened completely, trains terminated at a new station on the approaches to Liverpool Street named Bishopsgate Low Level. This was opened for suburban traffic only on 4th November 1872 and served as a temporary terminus until the first part of Liverpool Street was opened on 2nd February 1874.

The frenetic activity was not confined to the City end however, as work was now continuing apace with the line between Bethnal Green Junction and Walthamstow.

Bethnal Green Junction was a completely new station which opened on 24th May 1872, three days before the Hackney Downs route. It replaced an earlier station named Mile End, which was entered from what is now Cambridge Heath Road. By all accounts, Mile End was a fairly spartan place, offering little in the way of passenger comforts, but the same could not be said for Bethnal Green Junction, or any of the stations on the new line.

Curving northwards from Bethnal Green, the line passed through Cambridge Heath and London Fields before reaching Hackney Downs. Here the tracks divided, with one pair heading to Enfield and the other towards Chingford. The first section of the Enfield line opened on the same day as that linking Bethnal Green with Hackney Downs (27th May 1872), but it was not until 1st August 1872 that the link from Clapton Junction to Hall Farm Junction was brought into use and trains could be worked by way of the new route through to Walthamstow.

Although the track between Hackney Downs and Hall Farm Junction was double from the outset, that continuing to Walthamstow was initially single.

Walthamstow, which for many years has be known by the Post Office as 'London E17' was then an Essex village. It was centred around St. Mary's Church, although housing had already spread to Wood Street and what is now the High Street. New estates had also started to spring up between Grove Road and Orford Road, but the area still retained a rural character.

Photographs of Hoe Street station taken soon after opening portray a Walthamstow that one would scarcely recognise today. The single platform lies amidst fields with scarcely a house in sight. The horizon disappears behind rows of trees and only the station buildings with their decidedly urban appearance give a hint as to the area's future. Ironically, although Walthamstow itself has changed beyond all recognition, the station buildings at Hoe Street, or Walthamstow Central as it became some decades ago, still survive, together with their characteristic GER 1870s-style awnings.

As for the other two stations, St. James Street also boasted a single platform, but to reduce weight as it was located in an elevated position it was initially constructed from wood. Shern Hall Street however remains a bit of a mystery. Its single platform, in common with St James Street and Hoe Street stood on what was to become the up side, but with seemingly complete lack of photographic evidence, little can be said about its facilities. We know it had a gravity water feed for engines and this continued to be used for a while after closure, but as to the design of its buildings, if indeed it had any, we can only guess, until of course, future research provides us with more information.

The reason for Shern Hall Street's obscurity is that the station was only short lived, closing as it did on 17th November 1873, when the single line was extended to Chingford. Shern Hall Street, ideally placed for the old village centre was replaced by a new station at Wood Street.

Wood Street was followed by a rather flimsy little wooden station at Hale End, then finally the terminus at Chingford. Here the district was even more rural than Walthamstow and the lack of piped water to fill locomotive tanks initially proved a problem. This was overcome when the GER purchased a farm pond for the purpose, having received the farmer's approval by digging a new pond for his cattle to drink from!

Like Shern Hall Street, this was not due to last however, as within a short time it was also replaced.

With the route now more or less complete, traffic soon began to grow and the line north-east of Hall Farm Junction was doubled. On 10th August 1875, a decision to double the formation all the way to Chingford was taken and the job was put out to tender.

By now, the GER began to think again about extending its branch to High Beech and with the application still before Parliament, the company constructed a larger Chingford station a little to the north. This was brought into use on 2nd September 1878 when its predecessor closed. The new premises were a vast improvement over that which they replaced and boasted bays located either side of two through platforms. These were intended for when the line was pushed onward to its ultimate destination, but for the time being, the tracks only stretched for a few yards beyond their country end.

On 6th May 1882, the Royal Train conveying Queen Victoria travelled from Windsor to Chingford where a ceremony was held dedicating Epping Forest to the public in perpetuity. The train was formed of Great Western Railway stock and ran by way of Acton, Victoria Park and Stratford. At Victoria Park the GWR locomotive was detached and Great Eastern 0-4-4T No 189 took over. This must have been one of the smallest engines ever rostered to work a Royal Train, but the company rose to the occasion by turning her out from Stratford Works in an attractive shade of royal blue. It seems that the colour proved popular as a version of it subsequently became the standard livery for GER locomotives.

A triumphal arch, built largely of wood, was positioned outside Chingford station, whilst flags and bunting fluttered elsewhere along the route. Around 20,000 people used the branch to attend the event, and numerous locals stood in their back gardens to watch the special train speed by. On arrival Queen Victoria was met by HRH The Duke of Connaught, the Ranger of the Forest, and the Lord Mayor of London. The party then continued by road to High Beech, where the official ceremony was followed by a reception in the Kings Oak Hotel.

Surprisingly, the wooden arch, which was only intended as a temporary affair, remained standing until around 1900, although in 1890 it was reported as being *"a hideous eyesore... a collection of old sleepers in varying stages of putrification."*

Soon after the line was opened, the area began to develop, particularly around Walthamstow, where within a few years rows upon rows of houses had replaced the earlier fields. Walthamstow in many ways became the hub of the branch, with a locomotive depot and carriage sidings at Wood Street.

In the latter part of the nineteenth century, the ever-increasing amount of traffic using the lines in and out of Liverpool Street resulted in a period of widenings. The 1890s saw additional tracks being laid on the approach to the terminus, partly under the viaduct supporting Bishopsgate goods depot, and Liverpool Street station itself was substantially enlarged. In addition, an extra pair of tracks were added between Bethnal Green Junction and Hackney Downs, intended for services not booked to call at the two intermediate stations.

Whereas Walthamstow had become totally urban, Chingford continued to retain a slightly more rural air and became a popular venue for excursionists living in the inner East End. During 1920, 1,000 women were conveyed to Chingford in two special trains financed by the politician Horatio

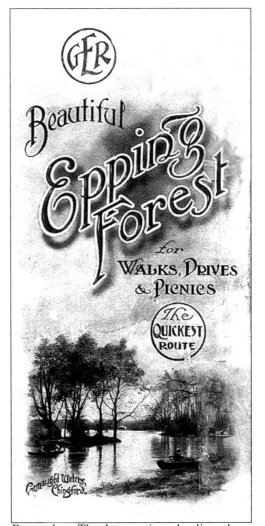

Bottomley. The locomotives hauling these each carried a shield headboard surrounded with five flags whilst the coaches were decorated with large red white and blue bows. The carriage doors each carried a letter, which collectively spelt out "Bottomley's Outing", although it seems that these had to be positioned by the Superintendent's personal train office staff to ensure there were no errors in the spelling! Events such as this clearly had a high profile, particularly as Chingford station was decorated with streamers proclaiming "Good Luck to Horatio", but ordinary, less publicised excursions also brought in a great deal of additional revenue. On Whit Monday 1920 for example, it is recorded that over 100,000 people arrived at Chingford and the company had to employ forty-six extra members of staff to deal with the crowds.

On 12th July 1920, the GER introduced a new intensive timetable for its suburban services in and out of Liverpool Street's West Side. To improve passenger flow and therefore minimise delays in loading, various modifications were carried out. These included a new arrangement of platform barriers at Liverpool Street together with a system of colour coding on coaches to denote their destination and class of travel.

A little earlier, the five piece Original Dixieland Jazz band had brought a wild and exciting new form of music to England and the word 'Jazz' became fashionable for anything loud or brightly coloured. Therefore, on seeing the assortment of hues displayed on the carriages the press came up with the term "Jazz Service" and this was soon in general use among the travelling public. Needless to say some people disapproved of such a frivolous title and, not wishing to associate themselves with jazz used the somewhat twee title "Rainbow Trains" instead.

The extension towards High Beech remained an unfulfilled dream and never materialised. The few yards of track which stretched north of Chingford station had been furnished with loco servicing facilities and continued as such until the end of steam.

On 1st January 1923, the GER became part of the London & North Eastern Railway. It was recorded that during the previous day a busker travelled back and forth along the line with a concertina leading choruses of *Auld Lang Syne*' and Ivor Novello's wartime hit *Keep The Home Fires Burning*'.

The 1930s saw the introduction of colour light signalling and, as a result of this, a number of the intermediate signal boxes were closed.

Apart from the effects of war damage, the line remained little changed when it became part of the nationalised British Railways at the beginning of 1948.

Electrification of the branch was first mooted in 1955 and within a short while preparatory work was under way. Further platform lengthening was implemented where required, but otherwise the stations themselves were largely unaltered. Electric trains commenced operation on 14th November 1960, but steam continued to work until the end of 1961 whilst various technical difficulties were ironed out.

At first the electric services were operated by what later became class 305/1 units, but these were later replaced by 315s and 317.

Following electrification various alterations have taken place, most notably with stations, all of which have been altered in some way or another. Goods facilities were phased out and the long-established carriage sidings at Wood Street were closed. To replace these, additional roads were laid at Chingford, therefore allowing stock used on the branch to be berthed there.

Under the rail privatisation scheme instigated by the Conservative government, the line became part of the West Anglia Great Northern Railway on 5th January 1997, the owners being Prism Rail plc. The franchise was was $7^{1/4}$ years.

The various changes have finally dispelled much of the Great Eastern atmosphere on the line. However, its trains continue to be well patronised so hopefully the Chingford branch will continue to serve its purpose for many years to come.

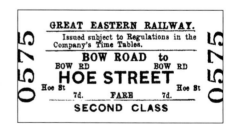

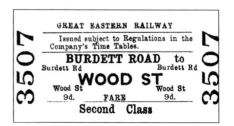

PASSENGER SERVICES

When the line opened to Shern Hall Street in 1870, the area around Walthamstow was still largely rural, so the GER felt that there would be no need for a direct link with London. Instead it provided a weekday shuttle service to and from Lea Bridge, which ran approximately hourly from 7am to 11pm, although, on Thursdays only there was an additional late train which departed from Lea Bridge at 11.43pm. At Lea Bridge, connections would be made with Bishopsgate services and with a couple of exceptions, passengers did not have long to wait between trains.

The Sunday service was less frequent, and was interrupted by the customary Church break between 10.30am and 1.30pm.

The opening of the route through Hackney Downs in 1872 resulted in a regular through service between Walthamstow and London. At first the trains were routed into the new station at Bishopsgate Low Level, but were extended to Liverpool Street two years later.

When the opposite end of the line was extended beyond Shern Hall Street, the basic service between Walthamstow and Liverpool Street became half-hourly, but the demand for Chingford was so low that a train every two hours was deemed to be sufficient. This was increased to hourly during the peaks, but it would be some time before Chingford truly became part of suburbia. Walthamstow was now steadily growing however, so the peak service to and from Wood Street had to be increased to every fifteen minutes.

The GER were quick to market the idea of Chingford as a venue for excursionists with additional trains being provided on summer Saturdays, Sundays and the newly created Bank Holidays. Sunday services were still subject to the Church break however, although by 1874 this had been reduced by thirty minutes.

Whit Monday 1874 saw trains running to and from Chingford every half hour until 8pm, and the little terminus was worked to its absolute capacity.

The opening of the new Chingford station and addition of a second track in 1878 allowed a more frequent service to be operated. Weekday trains now ran until midnight and certain services began to pass various intermediate stations without stopping. The Summer Sunday frequency between Liverpool Street and Wood Street was increased to half-hourly whilst the continuation to Chingford became hourly.

In July 1880, a service between Stratford and Chingford began to run at approximately two-hourly intervals. The afternoon and evening trains from Liverpool Street to Chingford began to operate every thirty minutes, whilst in the Summer of 1883, Sunday workings were introduced between Chingford and Fenchurch Street. These ran every half-hour and could be used by passengers holding cheap excursion tickets from the various intermediate stations. As they were largely intended for excursion traffic, it must have caused little hardship when they were reduced to two-hourly in the winter. The hourly summer trains last ran in 1888 and in the following year the service which had previously linked Fenchurch Street with Chingford was diverted to terminate at Forest Gate instead.

On 1st August 1885 a direct service was introduced between Highgate Road on the Tottenham & Hampstead Junction Line and Chingford. This ran approximately hourly on weekdays, although many trains were turned back at Wood Street and the service frequency was halved in the winter months. Excursion tickets became available over this route from January 1886 and in 1888, the trains were extended over the short distance from Highgate Road to Gospel Oak.

The development of the area around Walthamstow coincided with the rise in popularity of cheap 'workmen's tickets'. These were available for 'up' journeys on early morning trains, such as the 4.05am and 5.54am departures from Wood Street to Liverpool Street. Excursion traffic also continued to grow, but by the following decade some of this began flowing in the opposite direction. In the summer of 1890, special excursion tickets became available to Southend, which cost 5/- First Class, 4/- Second Class and 2/6d Third Class. No through service was provided however, so passengers had to change before reaching their destination. In 1895 day excursion tickets became available to Clacton, Walton-on-the-Naze and Harwich. Those wishing to use them had to catch the 8.05am train from Chingford to Stratford, then join a special which came down from Liverpool Street. Similar facilities continued in later years, although timings and routing details were changed.

The demand for trains between Walthamstow and London became such that in July 1897, they started running half-hourly through the night. These were mostly used by print workers employed around Fleet Street and others who worked odd hours. This situation lasted until World War 1, when the overnight trains were reduced to hourly.

Peak period services continued to increase with seven evening trains an hour departing from Liverpool Street in 1902. Among these was a pair which left simultaneously at 7.14pm, with one running fast to St. James Street, and the other calling all stations to Chingford.

The Sunday Church break was abolished from 1st May 1910 allowing a half-hourly Chingford - Liverpool Street service to be operated all day, although the Gospel Oak and Stratford trains remained as before.

The advent of war in 1914 led to inevitable service cuts and the closure of certain inner-area stations. Most of these subsequently re-opened however, although Bishopsgate Low Level fell into complete disuse.

Peak-hour overcrowding became acute and the GER had to devise a means of overcoming this. Electrification would have allowed a drastic increase in services, but would also have been expensive. Instead the company decided to improve its facilities and introduce the so-called 'Jazz Service' already referred to.

This was introduced in the summer of 1920 and provided the Chingford line with a remarkable off-peak service of a train every ten minutes. Various problems during that decade, notably those caused by industrial unrest sometimes resulted in the frequency being reduced to every twenty minutes, but otherwise the "Jazz" remained little altered until 1939.

The Gospel Oak services had been curtailed during World War 1 and although partially reinstated, fell into terminal decline. The old THJR single platform station at Gospel Oak was officially closed from 6th September 1926, but was pressed

back into use to handle Bank Holiday traffic until August 1939. There were also through workings between North Woolwich and Chingford during this period, although these were again largely intended for excursionists and eventually disappeared.

During World War ll, all that served Chingford were the trains to and from Liverpool Street and, as with the previous great conflict, the quality of service understandably declined.

By the 1950s, the route had again settled down to a basic pattern of half-hourly trains with additional operating during the peaks.

Electrification heralded the return of a ten-minute interval off-peak service on weekdays, although this was reduced to every twenty minutes in 1965.

In the autumn of 2002, the weekday service from Liverpool Street to Chingford commenced at 05.53 and continued until 00.53. For much of the time, trains ran at fifteen minute intervals. Services ran fast between Bethnal Green and Hackney Downs and therefore did not call at either Cambridge Heath or London Fields, which were served by Enfield Town trains.

1. Liverpool Street terminus opened in an unfinished state on 2nd February 1874 and was initially used for suburban traffic only. Much of its site had previously been owned by the Bethlehem Hospital, better known as the infamous Bedlam Lunatic Asylum, although the hospital itself, which had medieval origins, had been moved to new premises at Moorfields back in 1676.

The station was designed by engineer Edward Wilson and when fully functioning in 1875, occupied ten acres with ten platforms numbered from west to east.

Our view looks down the sloping approach and includes the West Side Suburban booking office on the left and the massive gothic-styled clocktower in the centre. (British Rail)

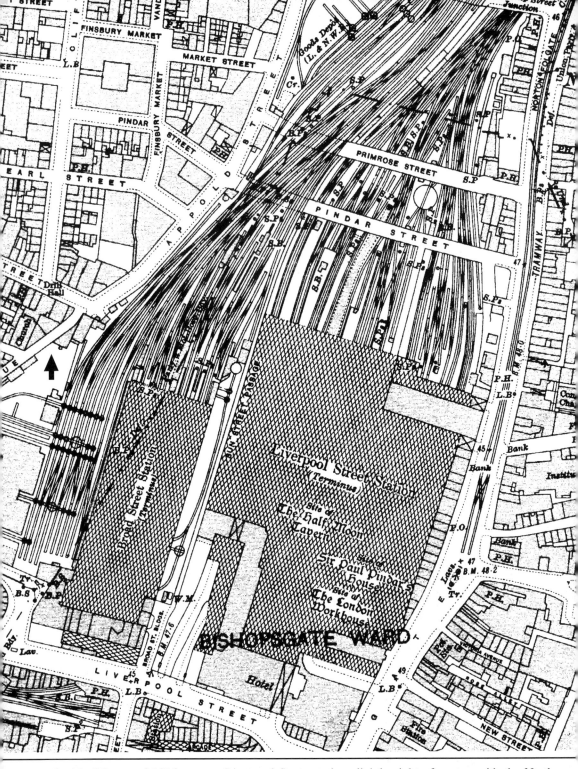

In this OS map of 1916, we see Liverpool Street station slightly right of centre, with the North London Railway Broad Street terminus to the left. Liverpool Street had been enlarged in the early 1890s, when additional platforms were constructed to the east of the site. These were intended for suburban trains serving Stratford and beyond, and were officially brought into use on 2nd April 1894.

2. Standing on the stairs which led down from the Suburban booking hall, we look towards the West Side platform barriers in the early 1900s. Beyond the arched wall in the middle distance lie the East Side platforms which were added when the station was enlarged between 1890 and 94. (J.E. Connor Collection)

3. A member of staff poses for the camera beside a destination indicator which was positioned in front of the gents toilet adjoining platforms five and six. The date of the photograph is unknown, but it must have been taken between 1903 when the Hainault Loop was opened and 1913 when services between Liverpool Street and New Cross by way of the East London Line were withdrawn. (The Lens of Sutton Collection)

4. A well-dressed man stands on platform 1, admiring the first of A.J. Hill's Class L77 0-6-2Ts, No 1000, about to leave with a train for Wood Street, Walthamstow, in March 1915. The locomotive is painted grey as were the majority of her classmates built in GER days, although No 1001 was turned out from Stratford Works in fully lined ultramarine blue. Part of the NLR viaduct supporting Broad Street station is just visible in the background. (KACR Nunn / LCGB)

LONDON, STRATFORD, and CHINGFORD.—Great Eastern.

Down.	mrn	mrn	aft	aft	aft	aft	aft	aft	aft	aft	aft		SUNDAYS. mrn	mrn	mrn	mrn	aft	aft	aft	aft	aft	aft	aft
Liverpool St. dep	8 5	10 0	1126	1225	2 10	3 15	4 11	4 42	6 5	7 0	54	9 50	....	9 5	10 8	1050	1258	1 55	3 10	3 58	4 50	5 50	6 50	7 50
Bishopsgate	8 7	1011	1128	1227	2 12	3 17	4 13	4 44	6 7	7 0	56	9 52	....	9 7	1010	1052	1 0	1 57	2 52	4 0	4 52	5 52	6 52	7 52
Bethnal Green	8 10	1014	1131	1230	2 15	3 20	4 16	4 47	6 10	7 0	59	9 55	....	9 10	1014	1055	1 3	2 0	2 55	4 3	4 55	5 55	6 55	7 55
Globe Road *	8 12	1016	1133	1232	2 17	3 22	4 18	4 49	6 12	8 5	1 9	57	....	9 12	1016	1057	1 5	2 2	2 57	4 5	4 57	5 57	6 57	7 57
Coburn Road	8 15	1019	1136	1237	2 20	3 27	4 21	4 52	6 15	8 8	8 10	0	....	9 15	1019	11 0	1 8	2 5	3 0	4 8	5 0	6 0	7 0	8 0
Fenchurch St. d	8 13	1013	1130	1228	2 13	3 13	4 13	4 045	6 13	7 45	9 32		8 12	9 12	1012	1112	1 12	2 12	3 12	4 12	5 12	6 12	7 12	8 12
Leman Street	....	....	....	....	....	....	....	....	....	....	....		8 14	9 14	1014	1114	1 14	2 14	3 14	4 14	5 14	6 14	7 14	8 14
Shadwell	....	....	....	....	....	....	....	....	....	....	....		8 16	9 16	1016	1116	1 16	2 16	3 16	4 16	5 16	6 16	7 16	8 16
Stepney	3 19	1019	1137	1234	2 19	3 19	4 19	4 051	6 019	7 51	9 39		8 19	9 19	1019	1119	1 19	2 19	3 19	4 19	5 19	6 19	7 19	8 19
Burdett Road	....	1022	1139	1236	2 21	3 21	....	4053	....	7 53	9 41		8 21	9 21	1021	1121	1 21	2 21	3 21	4 21	5 21	6 21	7 21	8 21
Bow Road	8 22	1025	1142	1239	2 25	3 23	4 23	4055	6022	7 55	9 44		8 24	9 24	1024	1124	1 24	2 24	3 24	4 24	5 24	6 24	7 24	8 24
Stratford	8 35	1040	1153	1250	2 38	3 38	4 38	5 4	6 30	8 13	1010		8 29	9 29	1029	1129	1 29	2 29	3 30	3 04	4 30	5 30	6 30	7 30	8 30
Lea Bridge	8 40	1045	1158	1255	2 43	3 43	4 43	5 9	6 36	8 18	1015		8 34	9 34	1034	1134	1 34	2 36	3 36	4 36	5 36	6 36	7 36	8 36
St. James's Street	8 44	1049	12 9	1259	2 47	3 47	4 47	5 13	6 40	8 22	1019		8 38	9 38	1038	1138	1 38	2 40	3 40	4 40	5 40	6 42	7 40	8 40
Hoe Street	8 46	1051	12 4	1 1	2 49	3 49	4 49	5 15	6 42	8 24	1021		8 40	9 40	1040	1140	1 40	2 43	3 43	4 43	5 43	6 45	7 43	8 43
Wood Street	8 49	1054	12 7	1 4	2 52	3 t24	4 52	5 18	6 45	8 27	1024		8 43	9 43	1043	1143	1 43	2 47	3 48	4 48	5 47	6 47	7 48	8 47
Hale End	8 54	1059	1212	1 9	2 57	3 57	4 57	5 23	6 50	8 32	1029		8 48	9 48	1048	1148	1 48	2 53	3 54	4 53	5 52	6 54	7 53	8 52
Chingford arr	8 59	11 3	1216	1 13	3 1	4 1	5 1	5 27	6 54	8 36	1033		8 52	9 52	1052	1152	1 52	2 56	3 57	4 57	5 56	6 58	7 57	8 56

* Globe Road and Devonshire Street.   b Except Saturdays.

September 1885

5. The tracks serving platforms one and two continued in a tunnel beneath the West Side Suburban booking Office and provided a connection with the Metropolitan Railway. This had been authorised by the Great Eastern Railway (Metropolitan Railways) Act of 1870 and was opened for passenger traffic on 1st February 1875. The connection was used by Metropolitan services to and from Hammersmith until 12th July 1875, when they were diverted to serve their own station at Bishopsgate. After this it was only used for occasional goods and excursion trains, with the last working taking place in 1904. The junction was severed three years later, but the tracks continued to be used for stock storage until 1916 when they were lifted. In 1914, the companies discussed bringing the connection back into use, but nothing materialised. This photograph, taken from platform one on 1st June 1920 looks towards the gloom of the tunnel and shows that buffer-stops had been erected on both tracks. Because of the tunnel, platform 1 could only be reached by means of the footbridge and therefore its barrier was located at a higher level than all the others which were accessed from the concourse. The West Side Suburban booking office can be seen above.   (British Rail)

6. A view taken from platform two on 13th July 1920 shows alterations which had been undertaken in connection with the intensive 'Jazz Service' which had just been introduced. The stairway leading to platform one had been rebuilt and an additional means of exit provided. There were now two water cranes instead of one as before and a more substantial fence had been erected behind the buffer-stops. The old tunnel leading to the Metropolitan Railway subsequently housed a staff canteen. (British Rail)

7. We look down from the footbridge in June 1920 and see the barriers leading to platforms two and three. The bookstall on the right was removed soon after as part of the scheme to enlarge the circulating area. (British Rail)

8. We are now on platform four and are looking back towards the buffer stops in 1920. The tunnel leading to the Metropolitan Railway can just be seen behind the stairway to the right. (British Rail)

9. This view, taken in 1920, looks behind the destination indicator shown in picture No. 3 and shows the gents toilet, which according to the sign, doubled as 'dressing rooms'. (British Rail)

TRAINS START
FROM THE LEFT

P. & O.
SPECIAL TRAIN

L'pool St St:
Nº 6 Ba
2 Jun

Nº 153.

10. Moving eastward along the concourse in 1920, we come to the entrance serving platform six. Part of the gents toilet is visible to the left, whilst in the centre, a board propped beside the barrier provides a reminder of when P&O boat trains operated from Liverpool Street. (British Rail)

11. We stand on the northern end of platforms 2 and 3 in pre-grouping days and see the North London Railway viaduct, complete with NLR train on our left, together with the chimney of the GER Norton Folgate power station to the right. The structure on platforms 4 and 5 was referred to as an 'observation cabin' and was provided because the visibility from the main West signal box was cramped and restricted. (British Rail)

12.   The alterations made to improve West Side barrier access in connection with the 'Jazz Service' of 1920 are very evident in this view taken two years later. Gone is the clutter portrayed in earlier photographs and in its place has been created a wide circulating area. We are looking down from the footbridge and can admire one of S.D. Holden's S69 class 4-6-0s in the foreground, which is waiting to back-out from platform nine after arriving with a main line train. Behind her stands No 1000, the first of the GER Class L77 0-6-2Ts which in LNER days were re-classified N7. (British Rail)

13. In this view dating from 1934, we are looking down the approach ramp from Liverpool Street itself towards the station entrance, as taxis await passengers from in-coming main line trains. The old West Side Suburban booking office can be seen adjoining the clocktower, whilst part of the ex-North London Railway Broad Street terminus appears to the left. (British Rail)

LONDON, WALTHAMSTOW and CHINGFORD—Great Eastern.

Down.	aft	aft	aft	aft	aft	aft	aft	aft	aft	aft	aft	aft	aft	aft	aft	aft	aft	aft	aft	aft	aft	aft	aft	aft	aft	aft
L'poolSt.d	5 2	5 8	5 16	5 22	5 27	5 32	5 39	5 45	5 55	6 2	6 11	6 14	6 17	6 25	6 32	6 41	6 44	6 55	7 3	7 10	7 14	7 17	7 25	7 33	7 43	7 50
Bshpsgate	5 4	5 10	5 18	5 24	5 29	5 34	5 41	5 47	5 57	6 4	6 13	6 16	6 19	6 27	6 34	6 43	6 46	6 57	7 5	7 12	7 16	7 19	7 27	7 35	7 45	7 52
BthnalGrn	5 7	5 13	5 21	5 27	5 32	5 37	....	5 50	6 0	6 7	6 16	6 19	6 22	6 30	6 37	....	6 49	7 0	7 8	7 15	7 19	7 22	7 30	7 38	7 48	7 56
CambdgH.	5 10	5 16	5 24	5 30	5 35	5 40	....	5 53	6 3	6 10	6 19	6 22	6 25	6 33	6 40	....	6 52	7 3	7 11	7 18	7 22	7 25	7 33	7 41	7 51	7 59
Ludn Flds	5 12	5 18	5 26	5 32	5 37	5 42	....	5 55	6 5	6 12	6 21	6 24	6 27	6 35	6 42	....	6 54	7 5	7 13	7 20	7 24	7 27	7 35	7 43	7 53	8 1
HcknyDns	5 15	5 21	5 29	5 35	5 40	5 45	5 49	5 58	6 8	6 15	6 24	6 27	6 30	6 38	6 45	6 50	6 57	7 8	7 16	7 23	7 27	7 30	7 38	7 46	7 56	8 4

Down.	aft	aft	aft	aft	aft	aft	aft	aft	aft	aft	aft	aft	aft	aft	aft	aft	aft	aft	aft	aft	aft	aft	aft	nigt	nigt
L'pool St. dep	7 57	8 5	8 10	8 18	8 25	8 32	8 40	8 55	9 3	9 10	9 25	9 32	9 42	9 55	1010	1023	1035	1048	11 3	1115	1136	1142	1155	1210	1210
Bishopsgate ..	7 59	8 7	8 12	8 20	8 27	8 34	8 42	8 57	9 5	9 12	9 27	9 34	9 44	9 57	1012	1025	1037	1050	11 5	1117	1138	1144	1157	1212	1212
Bethnal Green.	8 2	8 10	8 15	8 23	8 30	8 37	8 45	9 0	9 8	9 15	9 30	9 37	9 47	10 0	1015	1028	1040	1053	11 8	1120	1141	1147	12 0	1215	1215
Cambridge Hth	8 5	8 13	8 18	8 26	8 33	8 40	8 48	9 3	9 11	9 18	9 33	9 40	9 50	10 3	1018	1031	1043	1056	1111	1123	1144	1150	12 3	1218	1218
London Fields.	8 7	8 15	8 20	8 28	8 35	8 42	8 50	9 5	9 13	9 20	9 35	9 42	9 52	10 5	1020	1033	1045	1058	1113	1125	1146	1152	12 5	1220	1220
Hackney Dwns	8 10	8 18	8 23	8 31	8 38	8 45	8 53	9 8	9 16	9 23	9 38	9 45	9 55	10 8	1023	1036	1048	11 1	1116	1128	1149	1155	12 8	1223	1223
Clapton	....	8 21	....	Except Saturdays.	....	8 48	....	....	9 19	....	....	9 48	....	....	1026	....	....	11 4	....	....	1152	....	....	1226	1226
St. James's St	....	8 25	....		....	8 52	....	....	9 23	....	....	9 52	....	....	1030	....	....	11 8	....	....	1156	....	....	1230	1230
Hoe Street ..	....	8 27	....		....	8 54	....	....	9 25	....	....	9 54	....	....	1032	....	....	1110	....	....	1158	....	....	1232	1232
Wood Street.	....	8 32	....		....	8 57	....	....	9 28	....	....	9 57	....	....	1035	....	....	1118	....	....	12 1	....	....	1235	1236
Hale End	....	8 37	....		....	9 2	....	....	9 33	....	....	....	....	....	1040	....	....	....	....	....	....	....	....	....	1341
Chingford .ar	....	8 41	....		....	9 6	....	....	9 37	....	....	....	....	....	1044	....	....	....	....	....	....	....	....	....	1245

SUNDAYS.—Liverpool Street to Chingford at 8 33, 9 2, 9 32, 10 3, 10 22, *10 32, and 10 43 mrn.; 12 32, 1 2, 1 32, 2 2, 2 17, 2 32, 2 47, 3 2, 3 18, 3 32, 3 47, 4 2, 4 18, 4 32, 4 47, 5 2, 5 17, 5 33. 5 47. 6 2, 6 17, 6 32, 6 47, 7 2, 7 18, 7 32, 7 47, 8 2, 8 17, 8 32, 8 52, 9 3, 9 21, *9 33, *9 47, *10 2, *10 33, and *11 2 aft. * To Walthamstow only.

September 1885

14. With safety valves blowing and steam issuing from her Westinghouse brake pump, Class N7/3 0-6-2T No 69701 prepares to depart with a train for Enfield Town in the 1950s. (D.I.D. Loveday / The Gresley Society)

15. By the time this view was taken from the northern end of platform one on 13th August 1958, diesel traction had started to appear at Liverpool Street, although steam still reigned supreme on West Side suburban services and no fewer than four N7s can be seen awaiting their next duties. (R.M. Casserley)

16.   Class N7/4 0-6-2T, No 69600 (originally GER No 1000) blows-off impatiently as she awaits departure from platform two with a Chingford train on 13th August 1958. (R.M. Casserley)

17.   Looking in the opposite direction we see N7/5 No 69647 arriving from Chingford. The former North London Railway viaduct is visible above, complete with overhead lifting equipment which was used in connection with freight operations at Broad Street goods depot. (C. Carter)

AN ANNOUNCEMENT FOR ANYONE WHO MISSED THE LAST JAZZ TRAIN. NOW YOU CAN CATCH THE NEW JAZZ TRAIN.

Yes the Jazz Train's back!

From October 3rd the new Jazz Train
will run every 10 minutes from 10am to 4pm, Monday to Friday
and 9am to 7pm on Saturdays from the stations below.

The Jazz Train runs again for the first time since 1926.
And, once again, it will be the fastest, most frequent service
between Enfield Town and Liverpool Street!

It's the service you've been waiting for!

THE JAZZ TRAIN – IT'S TOO GOOD TO MISS

JaZZ TRain

With backing from the Greater London Council, the train service linking Liverpool Street, Hackney Downs and Enfield was increased in October 1983 and marketed as 'The Jazz Train'. The choice of title was perhaps curious, as by this time there were very few passengers to whom it would have meant anything. No doubt because of this, the British Rail Publicity Department produced a leaflet to explain the campaign. The result was a piece of colourful graphic design, which although eye-catching, chose to represent an ex-Great Northern Railway Class N2 locomotive instead of the more suitable N7. The fact that the illustration bore a strong resemblance to a model locomotive then being produced by the Wrenn company, even down to its bright green livery, hints that one of these had possibly been used for reference by the artist concerned. The route diagram at bottom left did not include the station at London Fields which had been closed since 1981 due to fire damage.

18. In the Autumn of 1983, a group of people are seen standing by the entrance to platform four beneath a banner which claims that 'Jazz Trains' were "too good to miss", although in reality they were formed of the same stock which had operated the route since the Chingford and Enfield lines had been electrified in 1960. (J.E. Connor)

19. Liverpool Street station remained little altered for over a century although it received damage in both world wars. This view, taken in 1983 shows the clocktower and West Side buildings which lost their roofs as result of an air-raid in May 1941. (J.E. Connor)

20. Here we see one of the West Side departure boards, which were erected as part of the 1920s improvement scheme and survived for more than sixty years. The station names were displayed in white lettering on blue vitreous enamel plates, fixed to wooden blocks, which were turned to list the appropriate stops by members of the barrier staff. The clockface showed the time of departure and would be changed once the train had left. (J.E. Connor)

21. In the late 1980s and early 1990s the station underwent a much needed rebuilding which greatly improved the passenger facilities. This view, taken in July 2002 looks from the walkway leading from the Liverpool Street entrance towards the West Side suburban platforms. As can be seen, the roof has been retained and has been skillfully blended with the modern additions which it now shelters. (J.E. Connor)

Other Middleton Press albums to feature this station are *Aldgate and Stepney Tramways*, *The East London Line* and *Liverpool Street to Ilford*.

22. Here we see the entrance from Liverpool Street in July 2002, with its twin brick-clad towers and attractive canopy. A bus station was created at the base of the building in the background. (J.E. Connor)

23. Clean N7/5 0-6-2T No 69665 blasts away from Liverpool Street and begins the ascent to Bethnal Green with a train for Enfield Town on 2nd October 1958. (R.C. Riley)

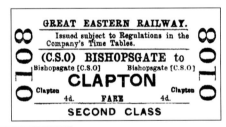

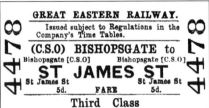

24. To provide electricity for improved lighting at Liverpool Street station and its other installations in the vicinity, the Great Eastern Railway constructed a power station at Norton Folgate. Design was carried out under the direction of civil engineer John Wilson and the plant was brought into use in November 1893. Often referred to as 'The Electric Light Station', it served its purpose well, but as the demand for electricity grew it soon became out-moded. A much larger power station at Stratford was therefore constructed during 1907 and once operational, Norton Folgate was reduced to the status of a sub-station. It remained as such until April 1932 when it finally closed. This view looks north and includes the 150ft high chimney above the Liverpool Street approach tracks. which was demolished in February 1934. (British Rail)

NICHOLLS & CLARKE LTD

NICLAR

GLOSS PAINT

SE & BLACKWELL'S PRODUCTS

TO SAY C & B TO YOUR GROCER

OLYMPIA

CAPTURED!

REID'S STOUT

PLAYER'S NAVY CUT

25. A siding was provided beneath the power station for the removal of ash and clinker. This view dates from the early 1900s. (British Rail)

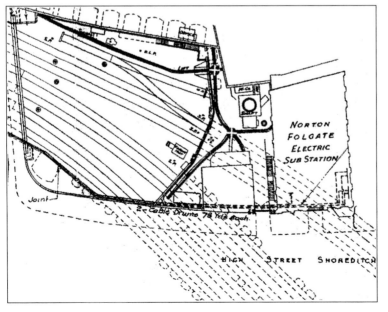

A diagram of the Norton Folgate establishment was produced by the LNER in February 1932 shortly before its closure. Waste products were moved around the site towards the chute shown above in tipper wagons, pushed by hand along a small internal narrow-gauge system.

26. After closure, the 'Electric Light Station' was stripped of its equipment and eventually leased out for non-railway use. By the late 1990s the surviving building had become largely derelict, but it was subsequently renovated and opened as a restaurant, appropriately named 'The Light' on 10th March 2000. This view was taken on 31st July 2002. (J.E. Connor)

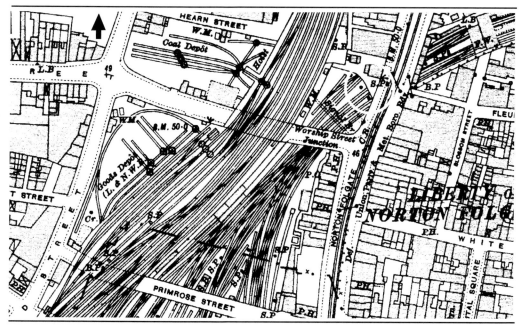

The location of the Norton Folgate 'Electric Light Station' is indicated by a white circle imposed on this Ordnance Survey map of 1916. The tracks heading north seen on the left are those of the North London Line, which since 1909 had been operated by the LNWR, whilst that curving to the east is the GER.

BISHOPSGATE
GOODS DEPOT

27. Bishopsgate goods depot was constructed on the site of the original Eastern Counties Railway London terminus and although still unfinished, was officially opened on 1st January 1881. This photograph was taken from the east end of Great Eastern Street in the 1920s or early 1930s. We are looking towards Shoreditch High Street and see the depot frontage directly ahead of us and part of its huge warehouse on the right. The tram visible on the right is obscuring the arch which once accommodated the Commercial Street Booking Office of Bishopsgate Low Level passenger station, closed in 1916. (J.E. Connor Collection)

28. The depot was provided with tracks on two levels. Trucks were lowered from the viaduct into arches below on hydraulic lifts, then moved around by means of capstans and wagon turntables. This view looks into the gloom of what was known as 'The Basement' and shows barrel roofing in the foreground dating from the 1880s rebuilding. (British Rail)

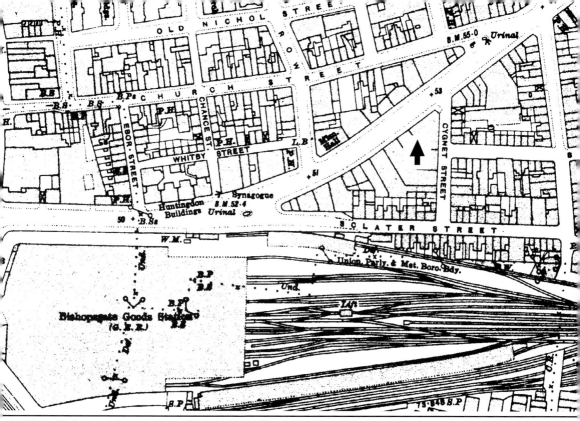

This Ordnance Survey map shows the bulk of the depot as it existed in 1914. The area immediately to the north around Old Nichol Street was a notorious slum in Victorian times and provided the inspiration for Arthur Morrison's renowned novel *A Child of the Jago*.

29. The facilities on both levels of Bishopsgate goods depot were very extensive. Here we see the 'fruit bank' which was located a little to the east of the main building and was intended, as its name implied, for off-loading fruit which arrived from rural East Anglia. (British Rail)

30. Here we have a 1920s view of the loading bay which was located at the front of the depot. As can be seen, horse drawn vehicles were still very much the order of the day, with that in the foreground being employed by the Co-operative Wholesale Society in Leman Street, Whitechapel. (British Rail)

31. The central section of the depot's viaduct was constructed under the direction of engineer John Braithwaite to support the passenger terminus of 1840. This photograph shows the distinctive styling of the original arches. (J.E. Connor)

32. A disastrous fire in December 1964 gutted much of the depot and resulted in its closure. The buildings were subsequently demolished leaving the former high level area as a derelict site, partially used for the parking of cars and lorries. (J.E. Connor Collection)

33. 'The Basement' fared better however and as late as 2002, even retained some of its track. There was also evidence of some old capstans and the site of two wagon turntables remained clearly visible. (J.E. Connor)

BISHOPSGATE LOW LEVEL

The passenger station at Bishopsgate Low Level was opened on 4th November 1872 and until Liverpool Street was brought into use, served as a temporary terminus for suburban trains.

It was entered by means of gates, located on the east side of Norton Folgate and the west side of Commercial Street. These served walkways which in turn led to a building above the tracks. From here, stairs descended onto the platforms in cutting below.

Being built on a restricted site, its platforms were staggered, with an island and side platform to the west of Wheler Street and a further platform to the east. The latter was used by up services and had its own stairway leading to an obscure doorway on the north side of Quaker Street.

A further entrance was established in 1882 when one of the viaduct arches supporting the goods depot was converted into a booking office. This was located to the east of Commercial Street and became known as 'the Commercial Street Office'

or 'CSO'.

As part of a suburban widening scheme, a pair of additional tracks were laid in tunnel beneath the goods depot and both of these were provided with platforms.

It has been stated in the past that the existence of this part-subterranean station resulted in all GER suburban tank engines being equipped with condensing apparatus, but whether this was the sole reason is perhaps debatable.

In its heyday there can be little doubt that Bishopsgate Low Level was a busy station, but the coming of electric tramways in the early twentieth century brought about its decline. When manpower shortages began to bite during World War 1, the GER decided to close some of its lesser used stations and these included Bishopsgate.

After some discussion, the date was finally set for 22nd May 1916 and, unlike some other stations closed at the same time, the abandonment of Bishopsgate proved permanent.

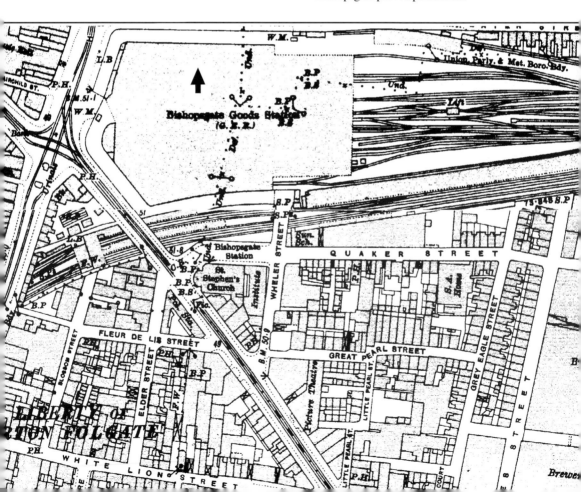

Handbill issued by the GER showing the stations proposed for closure in 1916. Bethnal Green was subject of a last minute reprieve and remained open throughout the hostilities. (D. Brennand Collection)

The Ordnance Survey map of 1914 includes Bishopsgate Low Level station immediate under the huge goods depot complex on the page opposite. Almost immediately to its east lay East London Junction, where connection was made between the Great Eastern and East London Railways. This can be seen on the section of map reproduced below, along with the ELR station at Shoreditch, which opened in 1876. The GER low level lines of 1872 are shown to the right, descending from Bethnal Green and passing beneath the original Eastern Counties Railway Bishopsgate viaduct, which was then only served by freight traffic.

GREAT EASTERN RAILWAY.

Closing of Railway Stations.

Notice is hereby given that on and from the 1st May next the following Stations will be entirely closed :—

BARKINGSIDE	GELDESTON
BETHNAL GREEN	GLOBE ROAD
BRADFIELD	LEMAN STREET
BUCKENHAM	LONDON FIELDS
CAMBRIDGE HEATH	MARDOCK
CHIGWELL LANE	SHADWELL
COBORN ROAD	STANHOE
EARSHAM	WEST MILL

The following Stations will also be closed for PASSENGERS AND TRAFFIC BY PASSENGER TRAINS :—

BISHOPSGATE	MALDON WEST
	TROWSE

H. W. THORNTON,
General Manager.

London, April, 1916.

50,000   Printed at the Company's Works, Stratford.   78087

34. From the Commercial Street Office a double-width stairway took passengers down into a passageway. From here, another flight led past an exit barrier to an adjoining arch which served as an exit. Those requiring up trains continued to the other end of the passage, but passengers wanting to reach the down West Side suburban did so by descending a further stairway. The arrangement is shown in this photograph, with the entrance stairs directly ahead, the foot of the exit flight to the left and the top of the down stairway to the right. (London Railway Heritage Society)

35. Having reached the bottom of the stairs, a snaking subway, lined in white glazed bricks, led to the down West Side Suburban platform. Here it is seen in 2001, eighty-five years after closure. (London Railway Heritage Society)

GREAT EASTERN BUILDINGS

36.   Numerous people were made homeless when the Great Eastern Railway enlarged Liverpool Street and widened its approaches in the early 1890s, so in an attempt to re-house some, the company erected a series of 'model dwelling' estates, or 'Artizans Dwellings' as they were recorded in official minutes. Despite their attractive sounding title, flats of this sort often provided their tenants with the most frugal of accommodation, although in all due fairness, they were invariably better than the slum properties which they replaced. Here we see Great Eastern Buildings which comprised two parallel blocks on the north side of Quaker Street, close to the company's smelly stables, and a short walk from Bishopsgate Low Level station. They survived into the 1970s, when this view was taken. The architectural detailing of the stairway top is similar to that employed on certain contemporary GER stations such as Bow Road and Maryland Point.   (J.E. Connor)

GRANARY JUNCTION SIGNAL BOX

Granary Junction was located near the Bethnal Green end of the viaduct serving Bishopsgate High Level and controlled connections to Spitalfields goods depot. The first signal box to bear its name was functioning by 1872 and remained in use until about 1880 when it was replaced. The second box survived until 15th January 1899, when a further cabin was commissioned. Sited on the north side of the viaduct, this differed drastically from the others however, as it was the first signal box in the country to be equipped with a power frame. This pioneering installation became the forerunner of the power boxes which can now be seen throughout the country. It was equipped with a 'Table Interlocker' frame, of a type first used in the USA and it worked both signalling and points.

37. Here we see the pioneering electro-pneumatic frame installed at Granary Junction by the company of McKenzie & Holland. The box remained in use until 9th October 1966, and although soon demolished, its historic frame was saved and now forms part of the National Collection. (J.E. Connor Collection)

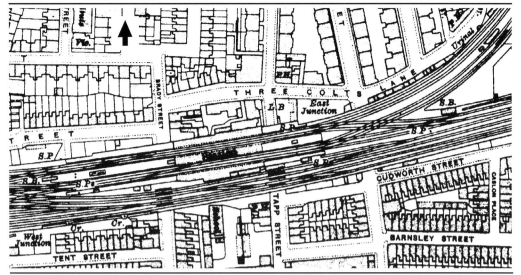

Bethnal Green Junction opened on 24th May 1872, to replace an earlier station named Mile End, which was located in what is now Cambridge Heath Road. The chief reason for this was the construction of the new line towards Hackney Downs which branched off west of the original site. No photographs or line engravings appear to have survived of Mile End, but according to a reminiscence published in the staff magazine *Great Eastern News*, the facilities were very poor and nowhere near as commodious as those on offer at Bethnal Green. This Ordnance Survey map shows the station layout in 1914 with the Hackney Downs line forking to the north-east on the right.

38.   Because Liverpool Street was constructed at a lower level than the earlier terminus at Bishopsgate, departing trains had to slog up a gradient of 1 in 70 before they reached the level of the original line.This photograph, taken from Bethnal Green West signal box shows an unidentified 0-6-0T nearing the end of her climb as she approaches the station with a train for North Woolwich. Some sidings alongside the high level route into Bishopsgate can be seen behind the up train on the left. (J.E. Connor Collection)

39. As opened in 1872, Bethnal Green had platforms serving both Main and West Side Suburban lines. The latter are seen in this view, looking eastwards in the early years of the twentieth century. In common with Bishopsgate Low Level and certain other local stations, Bethnal Green was proposed for closure in 1916, but a last-minute change of mind on behalf of the GER resulted in it staying open. (The Lens of Sutton Collection)

40. Class L77 0-6-2T No 1001 must have made an attractive sight in her blue livery when she paused at the station on 5th May 1915 with the 1.52pm train from Liverpool Street to Chingford. Bethnal Green West signal box, which is just visible on the left, dated from 1891 and remained in use until 13th April 1947. (K.A.C.R. Nunn / LCGB)

41. Grubby 2-4-2T No 7236 is seen at Bethnal Green with a train from Enfield Town to Liverpool Street in the late 1940s. The lamp posts still sport the white paint added to make them more visible in the wartime blackout, whilst the running-in board shows evidence of the word 'Junction' being removed from the station's name. The platform serving the up main suburban line, located out of sight to the right of this view was closed on 8th December 1946 and quickly demolished. (H.C. Casserley)

LONDON, WALTHAMSTOW and CHINGFORD —Great Eastern.

Down.

	mrn	mrn	mrn	mrn	mrn	mrn	mrn	mrn	mrn	mrn	mrn	mrn	mrn	mrn	mrn	mrn	mrn	mrn	mrn	mrn	mrn	mrn	mrn	mrn	mrn	mrn
Liverpool St. d	6 20	5 50	6 27	6 33	6 36	6 47	7 25	7 32	7 40	7 57	8	8 3	10 3	8 29	8 36	8 46	8 57	9	4 9 14	9 25	9 31	9 35	9 42	9 55	9 58
Bishopsgate ..	6 22	5 52	....	6 35	6 38	6 49	7 27	7 34	7 42	7 59	8	5 8	12 8	31 8	38 8	48 8	59 9		6 9 16	....	9 33	9 37	9 44	9 57	10 0
Bethnal Green	6 25	5 55	....	6 38	6 41	6 52	7 30	7 37	7 45	8	2 8		8 8	15 8	30 8	34 8	41	8 51	9	2 9 9 19	....	9 37	9 40	9 47	10 0	10 3
Cambridge Hth	6 28	5 58	....	6 41	6 44	6 55	7 33	7 40	7 48	8	5 8		11 8	18 8	33 8	37	....	8 54	....	9 12	9 22	....	9 40	9 43	9 50	....	10 6
London Fields	6 30	6 0	....	6 43	6 46	6 57	7 35	7 42	7 50	8	7 8		13 9	20 8	35 8	39 8	44	8 56	....	9 14	9 24	....	9 42	9 45	9 52	....	10 8
Hackney Dwns	6 33	6 3	6 36	6 46	6 49	7	0 7	38 7	45 7	53 8	10 8	16 8	23 8	38 8	44 8	47 8	59 9		7 9 19	9 27	9 34	9 45	9 48	9 55	10 6	10 11
Clapton	6 36	....	....	6 49	....	....	....	7 48	....	....	8 19	....	....	8 47	....	....	9 22	....	....	9 51	....	....
Walthamstw	6 40	....	....	6 53	....	....	....	7 52	....	....	8 23	....	....	8 51	....	....	9 26	....	....	9 55	....	....
" Hoe St..	6 42	....	....	6 55	....	....	....	7 54	....	....	8 25	....	....	8 53	....	....	9 28	....	....	9 57	....	....
" Wood St	6 45	....	....	6 58	....	....	....	7 57	....	....	8 28	....	....	8 56	....	....	9 31	....	....	10 0	....	....
Hale End ..	....	....	....	7 3	....	....	....	8 2	....	....	8 33	....	....	....	....	....	9 36	....	....	10 5	....	....
Chingford ...arr	....	....	....	7 7	....	....	....	8 6	....	....	8 37	....	....	....	....	....	9 40	....	....	10 9	....	....

Down.

	mrn	mrn	mrn	mrn	mrn	mrn	mrn	mrn	mrn	mrn	mrn	mrn	mrn	aft	aft	aft	aft	aft	aft	aft	aft	aft	aft	aft	aft	aft
L'pool St. dep	10 6	1012	1025	1033	1040	1057	11 3	1110	1125	1132	1140	1156	12 2	1210	1228	1232	1240	1255	1	2 1	10	1 18	1 25	1 32	1 40	1 55
Bishopsgate ..	10 8	1014	1027	1035	1042	1059	11 5	1112	1127	1134	1142	1158	12 4	1212	1230	1234	1242	1257	1	4 1	12	1 20	1 27	1 34	1 42	1 57
Bethnal Green	1012	1017	1030	1039	1045	11 5	11 8	1115	1130	1137	1145	12 1	12 7	1215	1233	1237	1245	1	0 1	71	15	....	1 30	1 37	1 45	2 0
Cambridge Hth	1015	1020	1033	1041	1048	11 8	1111	1118	1133	1140	1148	12 4	1210	1218	1236	1240	1248	3	1 10	1 18	....	1 33	1 40	1 48	2 3
London Fields	1017	1022	1035	1043	1050	1110	1113	1120	1135	1142	1150	12 6	1212	1220	1238	1242	1250	5	1 12	1 20	....	1 35	1 42	1 50	2 5
Hackney Dwns	1020	1025	1038	1046	1053	1113	1116	1123	1138	1145	1153	12 9	1215	1223	1241	1245	1253	8	1 15	1 23	1 27	1 38	1 45	1 53	2 8
Clapton	1023	....	1049	....	1119	....	1148	....	1218	....	1248	....	1 18	....	1 48	....
St. James's St	1027	....	1053	....	1123	....	1152	....	1222	....	1252	....	1 22	....	1 52	....
Hoe Street ..	1029	....	1055	....	1125	....	1154	....	1224	....	1254	....	1 24	....	1 54	....
Wood Street	1032	....	1058	....	1128	....	1157	....	1227	....	1257	....	1 27	....	1 57	....
Hale End ..	1037	....	....	1133	....	....	1232	....	....	1 32	....	....	2 2	....
Chingford ar	1041	....	....	1137	....	....	1236	....	....	1 36	....	....	2 6	....

Saturdays only.

Down.

	aft	aft	aft	aft	aft	aft	aft	aft	aft	aft	aft	aft	aft	aft	aft	aft	aft	aft	aft	aft	aft	aft	aft	aft
L'pool St...dep	2 2	2 10	2 16	2 21	2 25	2 32	2 41	2 49	2 55	3	3 3	10 3	18 3	25 3	28 3	32 3	43 3	47 3	55 4	24	4 14	4 25	4 35	4 45	4 48	4 56
Bishopsgate ..	2 4	2 12	2 18	....	2 27	2 34	2 43	2 51	2 57	3	5 3	12 3	20 3	27 3	30 3	34 3	45 3	49 3	57 4	4	4 16	4 27	4 37	4 47	4 50	4 58
Bethnal Green	2 7	2 15	2 21	....	2 30	2 38	2 46	2 56	3	0 3	8 3	15 3	23 3	30 3	33 3	37 3	48 3	52 4	0 4	7 4	19	4 30	4 40	....	4 53	5 1
Cambridge Hth	2 10	2 18	2 25	....	2 33	2 40	2 49	2 59	3 3	3 11	3 18	3 26	3 33	3 36	3 40	3 51	3 55	4	3 4	10 4	22	4 33	4 43	....	4 56	5 4
London Fields	2 12	2 20	2 26	....	2 35	2 42	2 51	3	1 3	5 3	13 3	20 3	28 3	35 3	38 3	42 3	53 3	57 4	5 4	12 4	24	4 35	4 45	....	4 58	5 6
Hackney Dwns	2 15	2 23	2 29	2 31	2 38	2 45	2 54	3	4 3	8 3	16 3	23 3	31 3	38 3	41 3	45 3	56 4	0 4	8 4	15 4	27	4 38	4 48	4 54	5 1	5 9
Clapton	2 18	....	2 31	....	2 48	....	3 7	....	3 19	....	3 41	....	3 48	....	4 3	....	4 18	....	4 51	....
St. James's St	2 22	....	2 35	....	2 52	....	3 11	....	3 23	....	3 45	....	3 52	....	4	....	4 22	....	4 55	....
Hoe Street ..	2 24	....	2 37	....	2 54	....	3 13	....	3 25	....	3 47	....	3 54	....	4 9	....	4 24	....	4 57	....
Wood Street..	2 27	....	2 40	....	2 57	....	3 16	....	3 28	....	3 50	....	3 57	....	4 12	....	4 27	....	5 0	....
Hale End..	2 32	....	....	3 2	....	....	3 33	....	....	4 2	....	....	4 32	....	5 5	....
Chingford ar	2 36	....	....	3 6	....	....	3 37	....	....	4 6	....	....	4 36	....	5 9	....

Saturdays only. *Except Saturdays.*

September 1885

42. Apart from the loss of its up main local platform in 1946/7, the station remained little changed for many years. Here we see Class N7/4 No 69603 arriving with a train for Chingford on 16th August 1958 (R.M. Casserley).

43. The canopies were rationalised in the mid-1960s and by the time this photograph was taken in 1981 the buildings were beginning to appear shabby. We are looking east towards the junction and can just pick-out a signal box in the distance to the right. This replaced an earlier cabin known as Bethnal Green East on 6th February 1949 and continued in use until 25th March 1989. (J.E. Connor)

44. Spring sunlight casts attractive shadows from the stairwell ironwork on the island platform in 1983, about two years before the station's original GER features were all swept away. (J.E. Connor)

45. Rebuilding took place during 1985-6. Here we observe the demolition work from a passing train and see that although the structures on the island platform had already gone, the down side building was still standing, even if stripped of its awning. A high temporary footbridge can just be seen, partially hidden by the signal on the left. (J.E. Connor)

46. Looking east on 31st July 2002 we see the replacement buildings which incorporate the stairways from street level. (J.E. Connor)

47. This wonderfully atmospheric photograph epitomises perfectly the character of London's East End railways. It was taken from an up suburban approaching Bethnal Green. The loco-motive, an ex-Great Eastern Railway 2-4-2T is about to pass one of Nigel Gresley's Class B17 4-6-0s, which is working an express on the main line towards Stratford. To our right we see part of an extensive estate erected by Alderman Sydney Waterlow's Improved Industrial Dwellings Company over a twenty year period from 1868. Waterlow, who chose to employ builder, Matthew Allen instead of a qualified architect to design his flats, was a prolific exponent of 'model dwellings' and a number of his developments remained in full use at the beginning of the twenty-first century. (H.F. Wheeller / R.S. Carpenter Collection)

June 1876

CAMBRIDGE HEATH

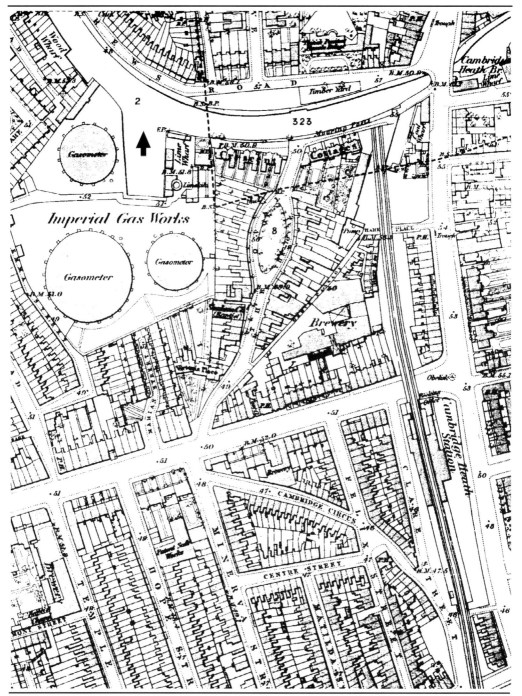

Cambridge Heath station was opened with the new line from Bethnal Green to Hackney Downs on 27th May 1872. It comprised two platforms and can be seen to the right of this Ordnance Survey map published in the year of opening. Interestingly, the railway is shown as terminating on the south side of the Grand Union Canal, therefore indicating that work had not been completed by the time the area was surveyed.

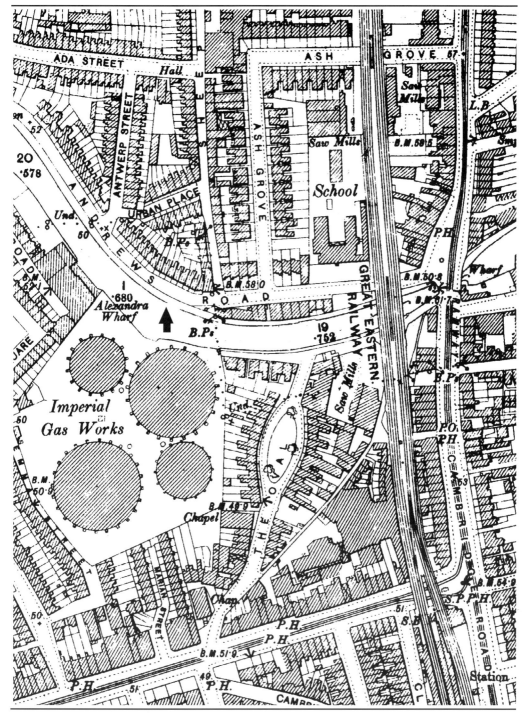

An additional pair of tracks were added on the east side of the viaduct between Bethnal Green and Hackney Downs when the formation was widened in June 1894, no additional platforms were constructed at Cambridge Heath, although a new street level building was erected to replace the earlier entrance. The revised layout seen on the Ordnance Survey map of 1916, includes the signal box, which was located at the station's north end and remained in use until 17th November 1935.

48. The station was closed as a wartime economy measure on 22nd May 1916, but reopened on 5th May 1919, seemingly no worse for its three years of disuse. This photograph, thought to date from the 1930s, looks north from the Liverpool Street end of the up platform. The additional tracks provided in 1894 are hidden behind the buildings on the right. (J.E. Connor Collection)

49. Still on the up side, we look south and see an N7 0-6-2T arriving with a train from Liverpool Street to Chingford. The station nameboard appears to be of GER origin and includes a supplementary sign advising passengers to alight if they wish to visit the East London Museum (now the Bethnal Green Museum of Childhood) or Victoria Park. (J.E. Connor Collection)

50. This delightfully evocative photograph was taken from an N7-hauled down train in the 1950s and shows the north end of the up platform before its vintage lamps were replaced by those of BR design. (J.E. Connor)

51. Apart from the erection of overhead wiring and replacement lamp standards, the station remained little altered until the second half of the 1960s when rationalisation saw the down side platform buildings being largely demolished. This view, taken soon after shows the up side, which for the time being, remained unscathed. (I. Baker)

52. The design of the street level building was similar to contemporary structures at Bow Road and Martin Street, Stratford, although there were of course detail differences. It was constructed largely of red brick and stood on the west side of Cambridge Heath Road, adjoining the junction with Hackney Road. This photographs dates from 1981. (J.E. Connor)

53. Not long before this view was taken in 1981, the up side canopy was removed, leaving the buildings looking very bare. Although these almost certainly dated from the time of the 1894 widening, the canopy was in the style of the 1870s, presumably to match those on the down side. Our photograph looks south and includes a small brick waiting shelter erected on the down platform to replace facilities lost during the 1960s rationalisation. (J.E. Connor)

54. On 27th July 1984 the street level building was gutted by fire and resulted in a period of temporary closure. The structure was declared unsafe and demolished immediately. Here we see engineers assessing the damage on the morning after the fire. (L. Bolton)

55. Cambridge Heath remained out of use until September 1984, then closed again between 17th February and 16th March 1986 for further rebuilding. This view shows the new street level entrance as it appeared on 31st July 2002. (J.E. Connor)

56. Very little of the 1872 station survived, although this fragment of building remained standing at the north end of the down platform when photographed on 31st July 2002. (J.E. Connor)

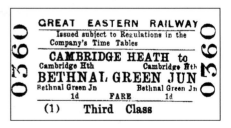

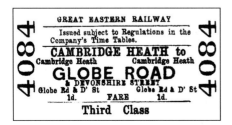

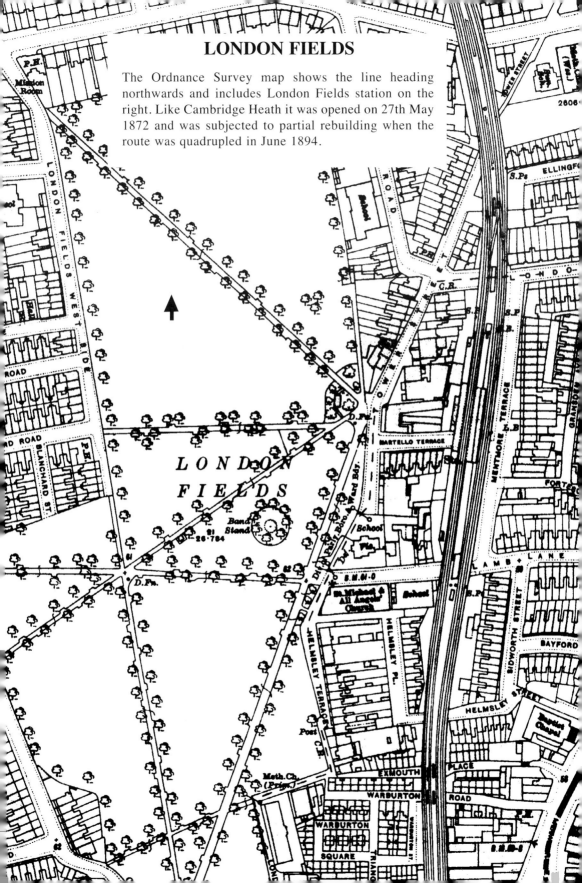

LONDON FIELDS

The Ordnance Survey map shows the line heading northwards and includes London Fields station on the right. Like Cambridge Heath it was opened on 27th May 1872 and was subjected to partial rebuilding when the route was quadrupled in June 1894.

57. In this view from the early twentieth century, we see an Enfield Town to Liverpool Street train arriving at the station. New buildings were provided to serve the up platform in 1894, but unlike those at Cambridge Heath, no attempt was made to match the canopies on the opposite side. Instead the design was typical of its era and displayed the type of valencing employed by the GER during the 1890s and early 1900s. The signal box just visible at the far end of the up platform was fitted with a 20-lever McKenzie and Holland frame and remained in use until 17th November 1935 when electric signalling was introduced. London Fields was closed as a wartime economy measure on 22nd May 1916, but reopened on 1st July 1919. (Charles Martin Series Commercial Postcard).

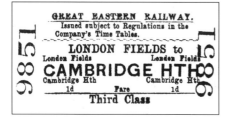

58. This northwards view from the 1970s shows that the up side canopy valence had lost its earlier decorative lower edges. That serving the down platform remained unaltered however and its styling betrayed its 1870s origins. (I. Baker)

59. Apart from the few minor changes already mentioned, the station remained little altered into the 1980s. Here we are standing on the south end of the up platform looking towards Hackney Downs in 1981. (J.E. Connor)

60. The street level entrance of 1894 was constructed within the viaduct itself and did not boast a separate building as did Cambridge Heath. This photograph, dating from 1981, was taken from the east side of Mentmore Terrace and shows the rather inconspicuous doorway which provided passenger access. (J.E. Connor)

61. Once inside the door, passengers entered the booking hall, which was largely located beneath the 'fast lines' of 1894. Here we stand on the opposite side of the barrier in 1981 and look towards the passimeter ticket booth and exit onto Mentmore Terrace. A British Railways white on blue enamel sign can be seen to the left, pointing towards the down platform. (J.E. Connor)

62. On 13th November 1981, the booking hall and up side buildings were gutted by fire, and the station was closed. This view was taken from the down platforms a few months later and shows how derelict and overgrown it had then become. (D. Nelson)

63. The down side buildings were little affected, although they soon started to appear rather forlorn. This view was taken from the north end of the up platform and shows that nature was beginning to assert itself with foliage breaking through the un-cared for surface. A white-on-blue enamel running-in nameboard can be seen to the left. (D. Nelson)

64. This view from the opposite side of Mentmore Terrace was taken soon after the fire occurred and shows that the entrance had been boarded-up with wooden sheeting. Up above can be seen the rear of the up side building with the majority of its roof removed. (J.E. Connor)

65. For a while it seemed that the station might have remained permanently closed, but following complete refurbishment, subsidised by the Greater London Council, it was brought back into use on 25th September 1986. This view looks north along the up platform on 31st July 2002 as a Class 317 unit passes on the opposite track. (J.E. Connor)

HACKNEY DOWNS

This station was opened on 27th May 1872 and enlarged four years later when centre through roads were laid. Further rebuilding came as a result of the 1894 widening and the finished result is shown on this Ordnance Survey map of 1913. At the top we see Hackney Downs Junction with the Chingford line diverging to the right and the Enfield branch on the left. Towards the bottom of the map lies the North London Railway, with part of Hackney station visible on the right and Graham Road goods depot on the left. Details of these can be found in the Middleton Album *Branch Lines of East London*.

66. The street level entrance was located beneath the bridge on the south side of Dalston Lane and comprised a doorway which led into the booking hall. This view, from the early twentieth century, shows the bridge and a stretch of 1890s canopy on the island platform, but not the entrance as this is obscured by the fruit & vegetable stall on the right. The well dressed lady concealing her face behind the dainty parasol adds a touch of Edwardian glamour. (Charles Martin Series Commercial Postcard)

67. This photo, probably taken around the same time, shows Hackney Downs station in its prime, with an Enfield to Liverpool Street train arriving. To the left we see the earlier 1870s awnings, whilst those on the island date from 1894. (Commercial Postcard)

68. Standing between the diverging Chingford and Enfield lines, we look south towards the station in pre-grouping times and see Hackney Downs North Junction signal box together with the 1870s down platform and 1894 island. The box was renamed Hackney Downs Junction in 1935 and remained in use until the end of May 1960 when it was replaced. The additional up platform which also dated from the widening is out of sight to the left. (British Rail)

LONDON, STRATFORD, and CHINGFORD.—Great Eastern.

Week Days / Sundays timetable (Down and Up): Liverpool Street, Bishopsgate, Bethnal Green, Globe Road, Coborn Road, Stratford (West Ham), Lea Bridge, St. James's Street, Hoe Street, Wood Street, Highams Park & Hale End, Chingford.

Sundays timetable: Willesden Jun., Gospel Oak, Highgate Road, Junction Road, Upper Holloway, Hornsey Road, Crouch Hill, Harringay Park, St. Ann's Road, South Tottenham, St. James's Street, Lea Bridge, Stratford, Hoe Street, Wood Street, Highams Park, Chingford.

July 1899

69. Looking north along the island platform in the late 1950s we see that overhead wires are in position above the tracks to the left in readiness for forthcoming electrification. All platform canopies have had the lower parts of their valences removed and the footbridge seen in photograph No 67 has also gone. A vintage lamp post sporting a BR type totem sign is visible to the right, together with an enamel running-in nameboard. (The Lens of Sutton Collection)

70. With her life drawing to a close, an N7 0-6-2T enters the station with a train from Chingford, and passes the power signal box which was brought into use in May 1960. (B.P. Pask)

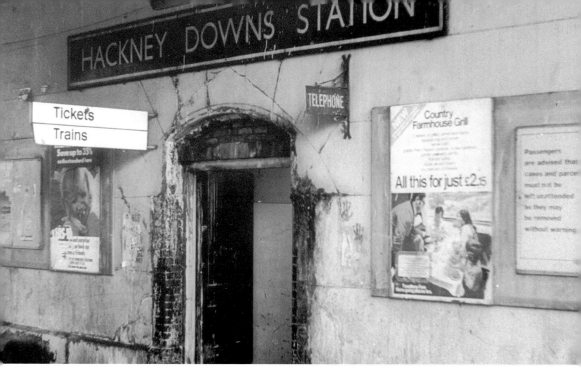

71. By 1981 when this view was taken, the station entrance was looking decidedly run-down, although the LNER white-on-blue enamel nameboard and the vintage telephone sign continued to provide a visual reminder of happier days. (J.E. Connor)

72. On the east side of the viaduct, south of the main complex lay this interesting structure which once housed an additional booking office. Dating from the widening, it replaced a slightly earlier facility which opened on 1st December 1885 for issuing tickets to passengers interchanging between Hackney Downs and Hackney on the North London Railway below. The two stations were linked by means of a covered footway which led from the west end of the NLR platforms towards the GER viaduct and the building seen here. The office was staffed by the Great Eastern, but it held stocks of tickets for both companies. The NLR prints showed the station of origin as 'Hackney No 2', whilst the GER issues carried the name 'Hackney Downs (EO)', with the initials indicating 'Exchange Office'. The building remained in use until the former NLR Poplar branch lost its passenger services in 1944. (J.E. Connor)

73. In 1981 a new building was constructed to replace the earlier entrance. This was designed by the British Rail architect Sandy Boal and was paid for by the GLC Urban Aid Scheme. The building, seen here in July 2002, leads into the earlier passenger subway which retains its white glazed brick facing and continues to provide access to all platforms. (J.E. Connor)

74. Up above, platform 4 retains its 1870s buildings and awning, as can be seen from this view taken from the north end of the island in July 2002. (J.E. Connor)

75. Platform 1 in common with the island forming Nos 2 and 3 was fitted with new awnings in the first half of the 1980s. However, the 1894 buildings, together with the canopy supports and stairwell ironwork have been retained, as is evident in this view, looking north in July 2002. (J.E. Connor)

76. We take our leave of Hackney Downs with this photograph taken from the north end of the island platform, beyond the signal box, on the same date. The Enfield branch can be seen curving to the left, but we will take the right-hand fork and head towards Chingford. (J.E. Connor)

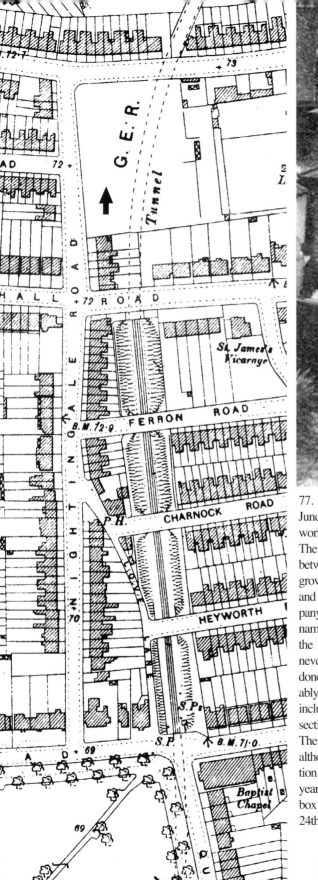

77. Soon after the new line from Bethnal Green Junction to Hackney Downs and beyond was opened, work started on a station to the north of Downs Road. The platforms were to be located within cutting between two tunnels and were intended to serve the growing residential area between Hackney Downs and Clapton. It was generally referred to in the company's minutes as Queen's Road, having taken its name from Queen's Down Road, which lay opposite the intended entrance. However, the premises were never completed, although they were not finally abandoned until 1895. This extremely rare view, presumably taken to show the signals, looks southwards and includes not only the 10-lever signal box, but a short section of what would have become the up platform. The platforms do not appear on the 1894 OS map, although a widening in the cutting indicates their position. The overgrown platforms survived for many years, but were finally removed around 1965. The box disappeared much earlier, having been closed on 24th February 1935. (G.W. Goslin Collection)

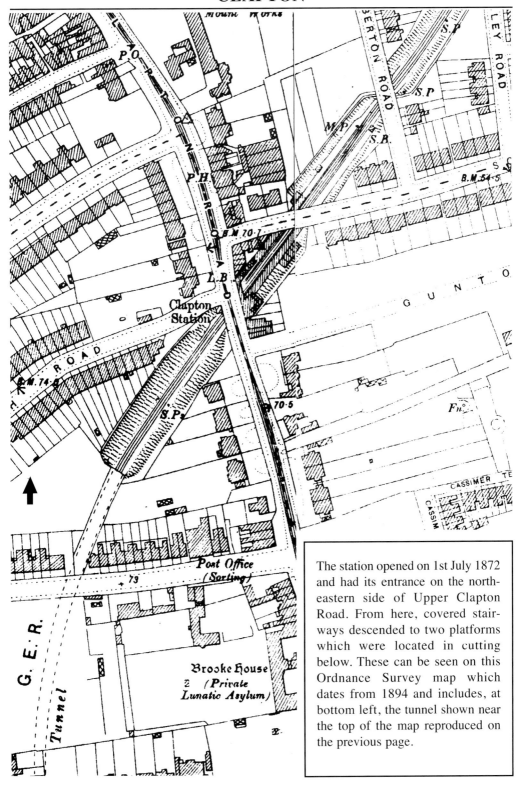

The station opened on 1st July 1872 and had its entrance on the north-eastern side of Upper Clapton Road. From here, covered stairways descended to two platforms which were located in cutting below. These can be seen on this Ordnance Survey map which dates from 1894 and includes, at bottom left, the tunnel shown near the top of the map reproduced on the previous page.

78. Here we see the street level building in the early years of the twentieth century with tramcars much in evidence. A GER poster on the right advertises three-shilling trips to Clacton which were available on Thursdays only. (Commercial postcard / The Lens of Sutton Collection)

79. A down train is seen arriving at the station in this scene taken from a Charles Martin Series postcard. This publisher produced a number of views portraying London area stations and, in some cases, provides us with a unique record. However, if a section of the picture was a little murky, or perhaps obscured by locomotive smoke, it would often be 'touched-in' prior to reproduction and occasionally the artist concerned made an error. Such a mistake is apparent towards the far end of the up platform, where the canopy valance looks as if it has been stretched downwards, with the lower edge of the final bay descending almost to the level of the platform itself! (Commercial postcard / The Lens of Sutton Collection)

80. Rationalisation of the station awnings began in the 1970s, when those on the down side were removed. Further changes came during 1982-3 when the old street level building was demolished and replaced by a new entrance, partly financed by the Greater London Council. The 1870s-style GER canopy on the up side was retained however and is seen in this photograph, taken from the entrance stairs in 1995. (C.D. Connor)

St James Street station opened with the original single-track branch to Shern Hall Street on 26th April 1870. A down platform was added when the line was doubled three years later and further improvements were carried out in 1875. This Ordnance Survey map of 1913 shows the premises in the form which they took from the latter part of the nineteenth century, with two entrances. The signal box at the west end of the down platform comprised 18 levers in its Dutton Trigger frame and remained in use until 29th January 1938.

Great Eastern Railway poster of 1897.

GREAT EASTERN RAILWAY.

NOTICE.

NIGHT WORKERS.

On Week-days, commencing Monday, the 21st June next, a Service of Passenger Trains will run half-hourly throughout the night between Liverpool Street and Walthamstow (Wood Street), calling at all intermediate Stations, viz. : Bishopsgate, Bethnal Green, Cambridge Heath, London Fields, Hackney Downs, Clapton, St. James' Street, and Hoe Street, for the convenience of Night Workers in London.

Return Tickets at Half Fares, with the usual minimum of 4d., will be issued by these Trains.

WILLIAM BIRT,
General Manager.

London, April, 1897.

PRINTED AT THE COMPANY'S WORKS, STRATFORD.

81. When opened, the only access to the station was from the east side of St. James Street, although an additional booking office was subsequently added to serve the opposite end of the station. Here we see the main entrance in the early 1970s, with a section of the down platform just visible to the left. (The South Chingford Railway Circle)

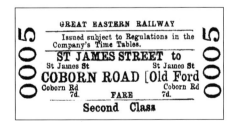

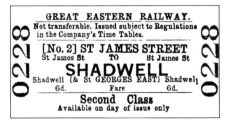

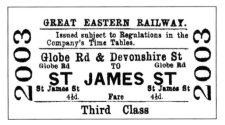

82. From the London end of the station we look north-eastwards towards Chingford on 14th September 1957. (R.M Casserley)

83. A photograph taken from the opposite direction in 1971 provides us with a good view of the down side stairway which served the eastern entrance opened on 27th May 1890. The up side stairs which led from the same building emerged beneath the canopy on the left and can be seen immediately behind the running-in board. (I. Baker)

84. Here we see the eastern entrance a few days after it was permanently closed. Its hours of opening were reduced in 1939 and remained so for the rest of its existence. Complete closure came in October 1967 and it was subsequently demolished. (J.E. Connor)

85. In 1974 the platform buildings were removed and a new ticket hall provided. The 1870s street level exterior was largely retained however and can be seen in this photograph taken in July 2002. (J.E. Connor)

86. This view looking towards Chingford was also taken in July 2002 and includes one of the new WAGN station nameboards, immediately right of the building, which were then being erected along the entire stretch of line from Bethnal Green. (J.E. Connor)

87. We take our leave of St. James Street, with this July 2002 photograph taken from the opposite end, looking back towards Hackney Downs. (J.E. Connor)

WALTHAMSTOW CENTRAL

88. Opened as Hoe Street on 26th April 1870, the station was originally provided with a single platform on what later became the up side. This view was taken whilst the premises were still fairly new and shows the space for a second track cleared in the foreground. When the railway arrived in the area, Walthamstow was still an Essex village, but within a short while its surrounding fields became submerged beneath a sea of bricks and mortar. (J.E. Connor Collection)

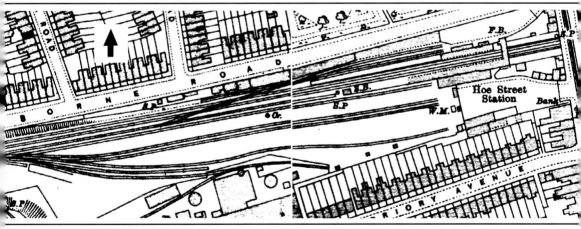

A down platform was provided when the line was doubled in 1873 although initially it is understood to have been devoid of buildings. This could be accessed by means of steps leading from Selborne Road, but the presence of adjoining coal sidings could prove hazardous to passengers. The coal yard, which subsequently also handled building materials, was resited south of the line on 15th July 1880 and seventeen years later a down side booking office was opened. This Ordnance Survey map from 1913 shows the station and its adjoining sidings. The line just visible at the left hand bottom corner is the Tottenham & Forest Gate Railway which linked South Tottenham with Barking and was provided with a station now known as Walthamstow Queens Road.

89. Class N7/4 0-6-2T No 69610 stands at Hoe Street on 14th September 1957 with a Liverpool Street - Chingford train. The footbridge dated from 1887 and was provided with a double gangway. The inner corridor connected the two platforms, whilst the outer was accessed from outside the station and was intended for pedestrians wishing to cross from one side of the line to the other. (H.C. Casserley)

90. A view from the opposite direction includes a glimpse of the timber yard which lay behind the down platform. (The Lens of Sutton Collection)

91. We move on to 23rd April 1960 and see that the wires are now in position for the impending electrification. Class N7/5 0-6-2T No 69656 awaits departure for Chingford. (H.C. Casserley)

92. Two old East Enders meet at Hoe Street. A pair of N7s are seen at the station in the latter days of steam, with that on the right working a train from Chingford and that on the left running light. The canopy seen behind the up platform protected the parcels siding which was incorporated into the goods depot. Although the yard was moved south of the line back in 1880, a couple of sidings were retained on the down side and were used by a timber merchant. These were lifted in the mid-1950s, but the main depot continued to be used until 2nd November 1964. (The Lens of Sutton Collection)

93. The frontage of the up side building appears to have changed little since its opening back in 1870, although the station was renamed Walthamstow Central on 6th May 1968, four months before it became an interchange with the Victoria Line tube. This view was taken in the 1960s, before the 'British Railways' headed poster-boards had been replaced by those of the corporate image period. (J.E. Connor)

94. We now view the building from its opposite end in the 1970s. The coming of the Underground resulted in a new combined BR and LT booking office being constructed on the down side, but much of the station's original character, including some of its awnings, have been retained. (The South Chingford Railway Circle)

SHERN HALL STREET

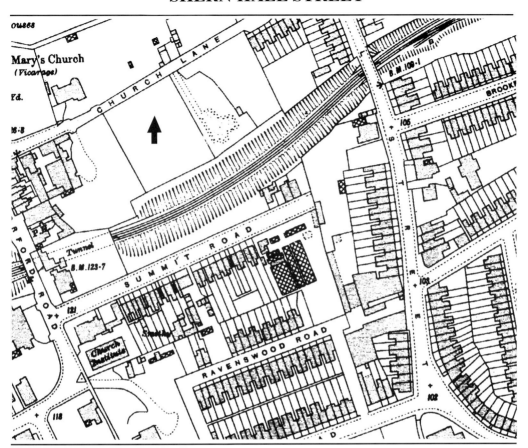

Shern Hall Street station was the original terminus of the branch and functioned from 26th April 1870 until 17th November 1873 when the route was extended to Chingford. It was located in cutting between Nag's Head Tunnel and Shern Hall Street itself and was entered from Summit Road. The single platform, which was positioned on the south side of the line, is understood to have survived, at least in part, until around 1921. Nothing of this is shown on the Ordnance Survey map of 1914 however, although it is possible that one of the houses backing onto the line at the east end of Summit Road *may* have been the former station building.

December 1870

WOOD STREET

Wood Street station opened as a replacement for Shern Hall Street on 17th November 1873 and can be seen to the right of this Ordnance Survey map of 1914. To its north lay a small locomotive depot, whilst to its south was the goods yard. This was brought into use on 20th April 1893 and closed from 6th May 1968. The connection with the passenger line was then severed and the sidings lifted.

95. We start our look at Wood Street with this 1930s view taken from the up platform as an N7-hauled train arrives from Liverpool Street. The large number of people waiting for it indicate that the picture was possibly taken at a weekend when many travelled into Chingford to enjoy a day in Epping Forest. The only person on the up side, which of course would have been very busy during peak periods, is an individual in Boy Scout uniform, who is seen walking towards the photographer thoughtfully puffing on his pipe. (Stations UK)

96. Apart from having its canopy valences reduced in depth, the station appeared little altered when this view was taken from the down platform around 1960. The lamp posts were still of the type seen in the previous photograph, but had been fitted with BR white-on-blue 'totem' name tablets. (The Lens of Sutton Collection)

97. Looking towards Hoe Street we see an N7 working a Liverpool Street - Chingford train. By this time the old lamps had been removed and replaced by concrete posts with strip-lights which displayed the station's name on their shades. On the right, an engineman is seen walking along the down platform towards the loco shed (B.P. Pask)

98. Still on the up platform, we now look towards Chingford around ten years after the previous photograph was taken. Despite the overhead wiring and new lamps, the station still retained a great deal of its pre-grouping character, although substantial changes were in the offing. (I. Baker)

99. The street level building survived for just over a century and its exterior showed no signs of significant change when it was recorded in 1973. By this time, the British Rail corporate image with its black-on-white nameboards had been in existence for just under a decade, so the survival of the earlier sign on the bridge was unusual. (I. Baker)

100. The Great Eastern buildings were demolished during 1974-5 and replaced by completely new structures. Here we see the replacement entrance as it appeared in July 2002. (J.E. Connor)

101. Standing at the London end of the up platform, we see the formation curving towards Walthamstow Central in July 2002. (J.E. Connor)

102. A view in the opposite direction taken on the same day includes the down side waiting shelter which was erected after the original buildings were demolished almost three decades earlier. (J.E. Connor)

WOOD STREET LOCOMOTIVE DEPOT

103. Wood Street depot was located on the down side of the formation, immediately north of the station. It never received its own BR code, as it was regarded as a sub-shed of Stratford and therefore its locomotives carried '30A' shed plates. This view was taken from the end of the up platform shortly before the introduction of electric services and shows an assortment of N7s waiting their turn of duty. (B.P. Pask)

104. It is understood to have opened around March 1879, having been requested by the Locomotive Superintendent the previous year. The depot was subsequently enlarged and in pre-grouping days provided employment for well over fifty men. At one time there was a coal stage, but this was removed by the LNER around 1934 as the company required its former site for two more sidings. After this, locomotives were coaled from wagons standing on adjoining roads. The shed was renewed many years ago, but by the end of the second World War was looking decidedly shabby. It was again renewed in the Post-War era then remained little changed until the depot closed with the end of steam in 1960. This view dates from 1957. (G.W. Sharpe)

HIGHAMS PARK

Opened on 17th November 1873 as Hale End, this was initially the least-used station on the branch. For over two decades the surrounding district remained largely rural, as can be seen from the Ordnance Survey map of 1894. However, in 1898, the British Xylonite Company moved their business from Homerton to a large purpose-built factory close to the line and the area began to develop. The station was renamed Highams Park (Hale End) on 1st October 1894, then Highams Park & Hale End on 1st May 1899. This name survived until 20th February 1969 when the suffix was dropped. The Ordnance Survey map also includes the goods depot, which can be seen to the left of the station. This opened in 1873 and remained in use until 4th October 1965.

105. The old station building is seen prior to its replacement around 1900. According to a Company minute of 1873, it was weatherboarded outside, lath and plaster inside and protected by a felt roof. (The Lens of Sutton Collection)

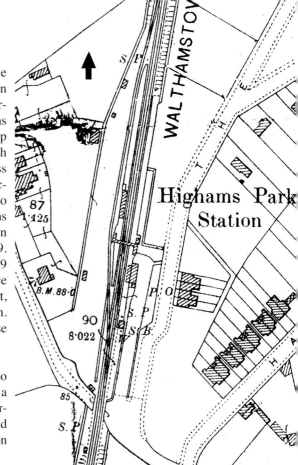

106. Even after the arrival of the British Xylonite works, the station and its immediate surroundings retained a rather rural appearance. In this view, an up train is seen passing the
brick signal box which dated from 1878 and was fitted with a 16-lever McKenzie &
Holland frame. The station building, erected to replace its wooden predecessor in 1900,
can be seen to the right. (The Lens of Sutton Collection)

107. Here we see the station as it appeared in the early twentieth century. The actual date is
unknown, but it must have been taken after 1911, because prior to that the platforms were surfaced with grit and clinker. Behind the down platform lies part of the goods yard, whilst in the
distance it is just possible to make out the top of a pedestrian subway beneath the line, opened
in June 1909. (The Lens of Sutton Collection)

108. Just before the end of steam, we look from the footbridge and see Class N7/3 0-6-2T No 69693 arriving with a down train. The canopy on the down side was lengthened in 1934 when an additional entrance was provided, although the additional valencing displayed the style of the 1890s/1900s to match what was already there. (B.P. Pask)

109. This northwards view, taken from the level crossing in the 1970s, shows the subway on either side. This was constructed to provide pedestrians with a safer means of getting from one side of the line to the other, although the GER and the Walthamstow UDC argued over its cost for four years before work could commence. (I. Baker)

110. Moving a little further north, we stand on the up platform and look towards the down side in the 1970s. By this time the goods yard, which closed on 4th October 1965, seems to have completely disappeared and its former site reclaimed by nature. The concrete footbridge seen to the right replaced its metal predecessor in 1957-8. (I. Baker)

111. Still on the up platform, we look southwards towards the level crossing and see the down side canopy which had been lengthened in 1934. (I. Baker)

112. The second Highams Park signal box replaced its predecessor in February 1925 and was located south of the level crossing. It was latterly used to operate the crossing barriers only and lasted until 2002. (J.E. Connor)

113. We conclude our look at Highams Park, with this view of the station frontage, which was taken in 1992. (J.E. Connor)

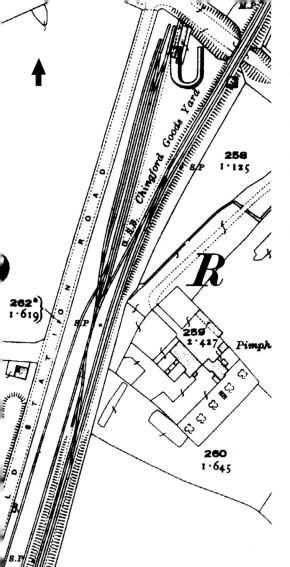

CHINGFORD (OLD)

The original branch terminus at Chingford opened with the extension from Shern Hall Street on 17th November 1873. According to the deposited plans it seems to have been intended as 'Chingford Green' but this name was never carried. It adjoined what was originally Hale End Road, although this was subsequently altered first to Station Road, then Old Station Road and eventually Larkshall Road. The station served its intended purpose until 2nd September 1878, when it was closed and replaced by larger premises further north. It was retained as part of the goods depot however, and can be seen as such on this Ordnance Survey map of 1894.

114. The old station building proved remarkably long-lived, and is known to have survived at least until around 1953. It occupied a single platform, which was built of earth and surfaced with grit. This remained in-situ into the 1970s, although in later years it was extremely overgrown. The tracks which served it were used as coal sidings for the yard which was located slightly to its south. This yard was closed on 4th October 1965 and was subsequently lifted. This view shows the derelict station in its final days. (D.G. Carpenter)

CHINGFORD

On 2nd September 1878, the GER opened a new Chingford station on a site north of the original. It was designed with the aborted extension to High Beech in mind, with two centre roads for through traffic and a bay on either side for terminators. A loading dock and associated headshunt was provided on the down side and the layout is shown on this Ordnance Survey map of 1894. In 1920 a group of carriage sidings were added, also adjoining the down line and this facility was subsequently enlarged when the route was electrified. North of the station, the tracks continued for about 75 yards towards High Beech, but here they ended. They were subsequently provided with facilities for servicing locomotives, but these were removed with the onset of electrification and the embankment was removed in July 1968, when the site was required for a new bus station.

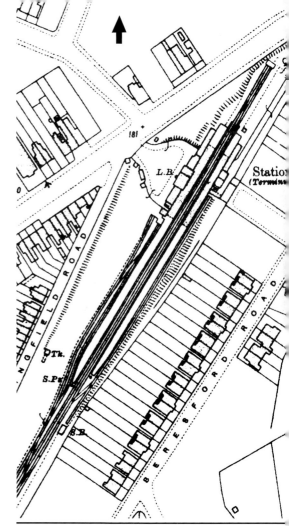

115. This fine view from the early twentieth century shows a line-up of people, mainly staff, posing on the down platform. The main station building is the double-storey affair which can be seen projecting above the canopy slightly right of centre. (J.E. Connor Collection)

116. The terminus is seen in the 1950s, looking north, with N7s very much in evidence. Vintage lamp posts can be seen on the platform, along with a white-on-blue nameboard which is unusual insomuch as it is fixed to the top of a single, centrally positioned, wooden post. Platform 1, the west side bay, appears on the left. (The Lens of Sutton Collection)

117. We move forward to around 1960 and see that the overhead wires are in position to power the electric trains which were about to take over from steam. To the right is platform 4, the east side bay, which subsequently fell into disuse. In the distance a light engine stands on the only stretch of the High Beech extension to materialise. (The Lens of Sutton Collection)

118. The main building retained an LNER canopy over its entrance for many years. Here it is seen in the early 1970s. (The South Chingford Railway Group)

GREAT EASTERN RAILWAY

Issued subject to Regulations in the Company's Time Tables.

CHINGFORD to

Chingford   Chingford

BISHOPSGATE

Bishopsgate   Bishopsgate
9d.   FARE   9d.

Third Class

2851   2851

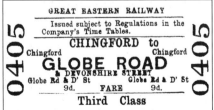

GREAT EASTERN RAILWAY

Issued subject to Regulations in the Company's Time Tables.

CHINGFORD to

Chingford   Chingford

GLOBE ROAD

& DEVONSHIRE STREET

Globe Rd & D' St   Globe Rd & D' St
9d.   FARE   9d.

Third Class

0405   0405

119. Here we see the up side entrance to the station as it appeared in the 1970s. Ten carriage sidings were laid out on the former goods yard site prior to electrification and a washing plant was also provided. (The South Chingford Railway Group)

120. Our tour ends with this 1992 view. We look north and see a walkway behind the buffer-stops. This was constructed three decades earlier over the course of the old engine dock formation and replaced a subway which had previously linked platforms 2 and 3. (J.E. Connor)

MP Middleton Press

Easebourne Lane, Midhurst, W Sussex. GU29 9AZ Tel: 01730 813169 Fax: 01730 812601
If books are not available from your local transport stockist, order direct with cheque,
Visa or Mastercard, post free UK.

BRANCH LINES
Branch Line to Allhallows
Branch Line to Alton
Branch Lines around Ascot
Branch Line to Ashburton
Branch Lines around Bodmin
Branch Line to Bude
Branch Lines around Canterbury
Branch Lines around Chard & Yeovil
Branch Line to Cheddar
Branch Lines around Cromer
Branch Lines to East Grinstead
Branch Lines of East London
Branch Lines to Effingham Junction
Branch Lines around Exmouth
Branch Lines to Falmouth, Helston & St. Ives
Branch Line to Fairford
Branch Lines around Gosport
Branch Line to Hayling
Branch Lines to Henley, Windsor & Marlow
Branch Line to Hawkhurst
Branch Lines around Huntingdon
Branch Line to Ilfracombe
Branch Line to Kingsbridge
Branch Line to Kingswear
Branch Line to Lambourn
Branch Lines to Launceston & Princetown
Branch Lines to Longmoor
Branch Line to Looe
Branch Line to Lyme Regis
Branch Lines around Midhurst
Branch Line to Minehead
Branch Lines to Moretonhampstead
Branch Lines to Newport
Branch Lines to Newquay
Branch Lines around North Woolwich
Branch Line to Padstow
Branch Lines around Plymouth
Branch Lines to Seaton and Sidmouth
Branch Lines around Sheerness
Branch Line to Shrewsbury
Branch Line to Swanage *updated*
Branch Line to Tenterden
Branch Lines around Tiverton
Branch Line to Torrington
Branch Line to Upwell
Branch Lines of West London
Branch Lines around Weymouth
Branch Lines around Wimborne
Branch Lines around Wisbech

NARROW GAUGE
Branch Line to Lynton
Branch Lines around Portmadoc 1923-46
Branch Lines around Porthmadog 1954-94
Branch Line to Southwold
Douglas to Port Erin
Douglas to Peel
Kent Narrow Gauge
Northern France Narrow Gauge
Romneyrail
Southern France Narrow Gauge
Sussex Narrow Gauge
Surrey Narrow Gauge
Two-Foot Gauge Survivors
Vivarais Narrow Gauge

SOUTH COAST RAILWAYS
Ashford to Dover
Bournemouth to Weymouth
Brighton to Worthing
Eastbourne to Hastings
Hastings to Ashford
Portsmouth to Southampton
Ryde to Ventnor
Southampton to Bournemouth

SOUTHERN MAIN LINES
Basingstoke to Salisbury
Bromley South to Rochester
Crawley to Littlehampton
Dartford to Sittingbourne
East Croydon to Three Bridges
Epsom to Horsham
Exeter to Barnstaple
Exeter to Tavistock
Faversham to Dover
London Bridge to East Croydon
Orpington to Tonbridge
Tonbridge to Hastings
Salisbury to Yeovil
Sittingbourne to Ramsgate
Swanley to Ashford
Tavistock to Plymouth
Three Bridges to Brighton
Victoria to Bromley South
Victoria to East Croydon
Waterloo to Windsor
Waterloo to Woking
Woking to Portsmouth
Woking to Southampton
Yeovil to Exeter

EASTERN MAIN LINES
Barking to Southend
Ely to Kings Lynn
Ely to Norwich
Fenchurch Street to Barking
Ilford to Shenfield
Ipswich to Saxmundham
Liverpool Street to Ilford
Saxmundham to Yarmouth
Tilbury Loop

WESTERN MAIN LINES
Didcot to Swindon
Ealing to Slough
Exeter to Newton Abbot
Newton Abbot to Plymouth
Newbury to Westbury
Paddington to Ealing
Paddington to Princes Risborough
Plymouth to St. Austell
Princes Risborough to Banbury
Reading to Didcot
Slough to Newbury
St. Austell to Penzance
Swindon to Bristol
Taunton to Exeter
Westbury to Taunton

MIDLAND MAIN LINES
Euston to Harrow & Wealdstone
St. Pancras to St. Albans

COUNTRY RAILWAY ROUTES
Abergavenny to Merthyr
Andover to Southampton
Bath to Evercreech Junction
Bath Green Park to Bristol
Bournemouth to Evercreech Junction
Burnham to Evercreech Junction
Cheltenham to Andover
Croydon to East Grinstead
Didcot to Winchester
East Kent Light Railway
Fareham to Salisbury
Guildford to Redhill
Reading to Basingstoke
Reading to Guildford
Redhill to Ashford
Salisbury to Westbury
Stratford upon Avon to Cheltenham
Strood to Paddock Wood
Taunton to Barnstaple
Wenford Bridge to Fowey
Westbury to Bath
Woking to Alton
Yeovil to Dorchester

GREAT RAILWAY ERAS
Ashford from Steam to Eurostar
Clapham Junction 50 years of change
Festiniog in the Fifties
Festiniog in the Sixties
Festiniog 50 years of enterprise
Isle of Wight Lines 50 years of change
Railways to Victory 1944-46
Return to Blaenau 1970-82
SECR Centenary album
Talyllyn 50 years of change
Yeovil 50 years of change

LONDON SUBURBAN RAILWAYS
Caterham and Tattenham Corner
Charing Cross to Dartford
Clapham Jn. to Beckenham Jn.
Crystal Palace (HL) & Catford Loop
East London Line
Finsbury Park to Alexandra Palace
Holbourn Viaduct to Lewisham
Kingston and Hounslow Loops
Lewisham to Dartford
Lines around Wimbledon
Liverpool Street to Chingford
London Bridge to Addiscombe
Mitcham Junction Lines
North London Line
South London Line
West Croydon to Epsom
West London Line
Willesden Junction to Richmond
Wimbledon to Beckenham
Wimbledon to Epsom

STEAMING THROUGH
Steaming through Cornwall
Steaming through the Isle of Wight
Steaming through Kent
Steaming through West Hants
Steaming through West Sussex

TRAMWAY CLASSICS
Aldgate & Stepney Tramways
Barnet & Finchley Tramways
Bath Tramways
Brighton's Tramways
Bristol's Tramways
Burton & Ashby Tramways
Camberwell & W.Norwood Tramways
Clapham & Streatham Tramways
Croydon's Tramways
Dover's Tramways
East Ham & West Ham Tramways
Edgware and Willesden Tramways
Eltham & Woolwich Tramways
Embankment & Waterloo Tramways
Enfield & Wood Green Tramways
Exeter & Taunton Tramways
Greenwich & Dartford Tramways
Hammersmith & Hounslow Tramways
Hampstead & Highgate Tramways
Hastings Tramways
Holborn & Finsbury Tramways
Ilford & Barking Tramways
Kingston & Wimbledon Tramways
Lewisham & Catford Tramways
Liverpool Tramways 1. Eastern Routes
Liverpool Tramways 2. Southern Routes
Liverpool Tramways 3. Northern Routes
Maidstone & Chatham Tramways
Margate to Ramsgate
North Kent Tramways
Norwich Tramways
Reading Tramways
Seaton & Eastbourne Tramways
Shepherds Bush & Uxbridge Tramways
Southend-on-sea Tramways
Southwark & Deptford Tramways
Stamford Hill Tramways
Twickenham & Kingston Tramways
Victoria & Lambeth Tramways
Waltham Cross & Edmonton Tramways
Walthamstow & Leyton Tramways
Wandsworth & Battersea Tramways

TROLLEYBUS CLASSICS
Croydon Trolleybuses
Derby Trolleybuses
Hastings Trolleybuses
Huddersfield Trolleybuses
Maidstone Trolleybuses
Portsmouth Trolleybuses
Woolwich & Dartford Trolleybuses

WATERWAY ALBUMS
Kent and East Sussex Waterways
London to Portsmouth Waterways
West Sussex Waterways

MILITARY BOOKS
Battle over Portsmouth
Battle over Sussex 1940
Bombers over Sussex 1943-45
Bognor at War
Military Defence of West Sussex
Military Signals from the South Coast
Secret Sussex Resistance
Surrey Home Guard

OTHER RAILWAY BOOKS
Index to all Middleton Press stations
Industrial Railways of the South
South Eastern & Chatham Railway
London Chatham & Dover Railway
War on the Line (SR 1939-45)

BIOGRAPHY
Garraway Father & Son